tips from your *Nana*

PIER 9

For my Nana,
Connie King, on her ninetieth birthday

Robyn would like to thank:

Kylie Sutcliffe and Jenni Long, whose assistance and belief in this book helped make it happen; Barbara, Nicky, Christine and Annette from Longacre Press, without whom there would be no book; Tammy and Katy, whose beautiful work makes this book what it is; Margot and Richard, who provided a sanctuary; both my parents, Jan and Fraser, for their emotional and practical support; Paula, whose love and support allows me to create. Lastly, my heartfelt thanks to all those who willingly gave their tips and ideas — those who are in these pages, and those who are not.

Tammy would like to thank:

My parents, Duncan and Jean, and my sister Kim, for their constant encouragement and support for my photography; my husband Marty, for his endless patience and love; Vic, my amazing assistant on this book and a nana before her years; Melissa and Toby and all my other beautiful friends for their advice and adoration. Lastly, a huge thank you to Robyn for this wonderful opportunity.

tips from your Nana

Waste not, Want not!

Robyn Paterson

photography by **Tammy Williams**

Published in 2011 by Murdoch Books Pty Limited.
First published by Longacre Press, 30 Moray Place, Dunedin, New Zealand

Murdoch Books Australia
Pier 8/9
23 Hickson Road
Millers Point NSW 2000
Phone: +61 (0) 2 8220 2000
Fax: +61 (0) 2 8220 2558
www.murdochbooks.com.au

National Library of Australia Cataloguing-in-Publication entry

Author: Paterson, Robyn.

Title: Tips from your nana / Robyn Paterson.

ISBN: 9781742663593 (pbk.)

Subjects: Home economics--Handbooks, manuals, etc.
Grandmothers.

Dewey Number: 640.41

Printed in China

Contents

Those of us living in the so-called western world have been looking at life a little differently of late. Turns out those hippies were right after all — building a society based on buying stuff and chucking it out hasn't left us in a great place. The planet's prognosis isn't too rosy, a few men in suits have ended up with all the money, and it seems most of our favourite foods are toxic.

Tips from your Nana is designed to empower you, with a minimum of effort on your part. It will help you save the environment, it will help you save society, and better yet — let's face it, we're children of our time — it will help you save money.

Hidden in pockets of our world are people who still know how to do stuff. Some of them remember the Great Depression, or a few of the

Introduction

Nana told us this would happen: 'Waste not, want not,' she said, knowingly. She also gave us strange homemade things inside jars sealed with tartan fabric and a rubber band. We didn't pay much attention to that either.

But now we're starting to wonder what was in those jars and how it was made. We're looking sideways at the apple tree in the park and thinking, Maybe I don't need supermarket baby food after all. We're wishing we didn't have to fork out more money for a card than the price of the present, or pay someone else to take our waste away, then go out and buy a bag of compost. 'Surely I could do that myself,' we cry, 'if only I knew how!'

not-so-great depressions since. Some of them were original greenies back in the day. Some of them are bright, young Gen-Y types who realised self-sufficiency was cool again before the rest of us did; others grew up in countries where 'supermarkets' and 'supplies' were foreign concepts. Many of them have been brought together in this book to show you how to do a range of basic things in a straightforward way — without complicated equipment or ingredients. From growing organic veges, to turning them into preserves, to throwing the scraps to your happy backyard chickens — *you can do it!*

CHAPTER ONE

In the Garden

Sister Loyola's COMPOST

Sister Loyola Galvin

People come from far and wide to see Sister Loyola Galvin's vege garden. Its bounty feeds twenty hungry nuns, with leftovers! Sister Loyola took up gardening in her late seventies when she was asked, for the first time since taking her vows, what she would like to do. After several decades of service as a nurse and carer, Sister Loyola returned to a love of gardening that had begun with her father.

As a child Sister Loyola suffered from osteomyelitis — a bone infection — which confined her to crutches. Instead of being sent to boarding school like her sister, she stayed at home with her father and followed him daily in the garden as he tended his veges. Now, she says, he still gardens with her 'from heaven'. She, and he, really know what they are talking about — at a sprightly eighty-six years old, Sister Loyola won the coveted New Zealand Gardener of the Year Award. She is in no doubt about what makes a successful vege garden: 'Compost is my big thing.'

TIP: Gardening guides will often tell you to wash seaweed first to get rid of the salt, but Sister Loyola says not to bother! Our soils are generally low in minerals these days and the salt will do them good, not harm. Plus it's less work — always a bonus.

compost preparation

1) Get yourself a compost bin. The less adventurous can buy one from a garden or hardware store, but Sister Loyola builds her own by nailing planks of untreated wood together to create a box. And, really, if a tiny eighty-six-year-old nun can do it, so can you! Whatever you end up with ideally should measure about one metre by one metre by one metre. An excellent no-building-skills option is to lash four recycled wooden pallets together at the corners. These are often disposed of by supermarkets and other large retail outlets.

2) If you have built your bin directly onto the ground, line the bottom with a layer of cardboard.

'recipe'

3) Start your compost with a layer of rough twigs — small enough to break down. This 'roughage' is going to give your compost some breathing space, allowing the air to circulate.

4) Next, add a layer of fallen leaves. If you don't have any in your garden, it's a good excuse for a 'refreshing bush walk'. Give your family or flatmates a bag each and make them come foraging!

5) If you're lucky enough to live near a beach, seaweed is excellent for compost. Gather up a layer of the lighter stuff like sea lettuce (nothing too rubbery), chop it up with a spade, and add it to the bin.

Sister says: 'Chopped seaweed is also great to throw straight onto the garden around your growing veges.'

6) A layer of horse or cow manure makes for wonderful compost — Sister Loyola is a big fan of manure. If you live in the country, manure should be easy to access — you probably stepped in some this morning. If you live in a city it's trickier; but, if there's a zoo nearby, you might be able to get bags of 'Zoodoo' — manure collected from hoofed animals such as zebra and antelope. I like doing this: it's cheap, they deliver, and it makes my compost seem exotic. Chicken, rabbit and guinea pig poo are all good too.

7) Now that you've created a great base for your compost, you can begin alternating 'green' and 'brown' layers. Greens provide nitrogen, while browns provide carbon. The combination is important, and alternating the layers will maintain the balance of nutrients.

Sister says: 'Think of your compost like a club sandwich — keep the layers going, and alternate the colours!'

TIP: Make sure that whatever you add is well chopped, so it breaks down more quickly.

TIP: Sister Loyola uses pieces of old wet carpet to cover her compost bins, as they're great for keeping things damp and are heavy enough to stay put in the wind. Off-cuts should be relatively easy to come by at carpet stores or recycling depots.

GREENS

Greens include stalks and ends from the kitchen; the broccoli you forgot to eat at the bottom of your fridge; the broad bean plant you just pulled up; grass clippings (light layer only, maximum ten centimetres); and seaweed. Also coffee grounds and manure, which look brown, are technically a 'green'. Both are excellent for compost.

BROWNS

Browns include fallen leaves; twigs; hay; moist sawdust from untreated wood; shredded cardboard and newspaper; and lint from the dryer.

8) Moisten your compost with water, and cover it to keep the moisture in and to protect it from the elements. Worms should naturally appear in your compost and will make it rich in nutrients — look after them by maintaining a good moisture balance.

Sister says: Worms are not amphibians — don't give them a swimming pool, but don't let them dry out either!

TURNING

The idea of having to turn compost makes the whole thing seem rather tedious and, if you're like me, may have stopped you getting round to composting at all. The good news is this: if you follow Sister Loyola's compost 'recipe', keeping a good moisture balance and not forgetting to add rougher layers such as twigs, hay or sawdust now and then to let the air in, you won't need to turn it. It may end up a little chunkier than the stuff you'd buy at a garden store, but it'll work just as well and, hey, no one's judging!

9) After about four months, depending on how well you chopped your ingredients, your compost should be ready to use. Stick your hand or a spade into the middle. If you pull out dark, crumbly material that doesn't resemble any of the items you put in, it's ready to go.

10) Apply the compost to your existing garden, or start a luscious vege patch by sowing directly into the compost — voilà, your compost bin becomes a fertile raised bed!

TIP: If you live in a windy spot and you're quite small, make sure you weigh yourself down when gardening. Sister Loyola once got blown clean off the side of a bank. It put her in a wheelchair for several months, but she got an electric one so she could still get around the garden.

WHAT NOT TO COMPOST

• Tomato plants — these can carry plant diseases.
• Weeds — unless you want to grow a weed garden!
• Pumpkin or squash vines — these take over a year to break down.
• Food — food scraps, except raw vege or fruit bits, will make the compost smell and will attract pests such as rats. Save it for the worm farm!
• Citrus fruit — it is too high in acid, and the concentration of citrus oils means peelings take years to break down. Worms aren't so keen on citrus either.

Down on Dave's Worm Farm

Dave Armstrong has been selling worms for nearly a quarter of a century, but he has noticed a spike in business lately. Sales are high, and increasing steadily, as more and more people discover the benefits of having a bunch of hungry worms chew through their household waste and turn it into fertiliser. For Dave, worm farming was supposed to be a retirement hobby, but now it's a tough job keeping up with demand!

Worms are amazing little creatures whose digestive system produces castings (or poo) that's four times higher in nutrients than regular compost. This alone makes a worm farm a great asset for a vege grower. Better yet, a small worm farm can be kept inside — making it a handy alternative to a compost heap for apartment dwellers. Once established, a thriving wormery can get through almost all the kitchen waste from an average family, and if looked after, worm farms won't smell or attract insects.

Readymade worm farms are now commonly available from garden stores, but they can be fairly pricey. If you're watching your pennies or you prefer to do your own thing, it's easy to start a worm farm from everyday items — and it doesn't need to cost a fortune.

build a farm

1) Find two plastic boxes of the same size. Stackable storage boxes are ideal, but even ice cream containers will do the trick — and they're a compact option if you're pushed for space.

2) Create several holes in the lid of one box with a drill or hammer and nail, and several more holes in the bottom. The number of holes will depend on the size of your box, but aim for one every five centimetres or so.

3) Shred an old newspaper into strips; scrunch up the strips and place them lightly inside the box until it's about half full. Sprinkle the paper with water to make it moist, but not dripping wet.

4) Stack your 'holey' box inside the other one, raising it off the bottom using old blocks, upturned pots or whatever you can find. This allows the air to circulate and liquid fertiliser (or worm wee) to drain and collect in the bottom box. Make sure it is sitting level.

5) Add your worms!

6) Sprinkle some food scraps into the box as a starter feed, and tuck your worms into their new home by placing a bit more shredded newspaper on top.

7) Cover with a piece of wet carpet or fabric if available, or else with some pages of wet newspaper. This keeps the light out and the moisture in — just how worms like it.

8) Put the lid on the box and leave the worms to do their thing.

TIP: Check your box regularly to make sure it's moist. If it seems a little dry, sprinkle some extra water inside.

17

finding worms

The best worms for the job are tiger worms — so named because of their distinctive stripes. Don't pluck unsuspecting garden worms out of your vege patch, as they won't give you the results you're looking for. Tiger worms can be bought from some garden stores or through private worm farmers like Dave. Alternatively you can siphon a few from a friend's worm farm to get yours started. Once settled, your worms will breed to fill the space you give them, and won't overpopulate. About a thousand worms (250 grams) is a good starting stock for a family farm.

WHAT WORMS LIKE
· Most fruit and vege scraps.
· Waste from juicers (unless citrus).
· Paper and tissues.
· Cardboard boxes (soaked and ripped into small bits).
· Hair from hairbrushes (off-putting, but true!).
· Coffee grounds.
· Egg shells.
· Leaves.
· Banana skins (a favourite worm treat).

TIP: Feed your worms about once a week, depending on how quickly they're getting through what you give them. This may vary a little from season to season.

TIP: Although worms have a surprisingly diverse diet, remember that they're tiny and don't have teeth - so break their feed into small pieces.

WHAT WORMS DON'T LIKE
· Very acidic foods like citrus, tomato or kiwifruit.
· Onion skins.
· Dairy products.
· Pasta and bread.
· Meat.
· Spicy food.

harvesting

About four times a year, harvest the fertiliser generated by the worms and refresh their bedding. There are several ways of doing this:

1) Get right in there and scoop off the top half of your box's contents, which will contain most of the worms. Put this half safely aside, and empty out the rest for use in your garden or pot plants. Replace the wormy half, and top it up with new food and bedding.

TIP: Bury their food just below the surface of their bedding, as they don't like poking their little heads up into the open air. It's all a bit scary for them.

2) The less-worm-touching version of this is to push the contents of the box to one side, and fill the other side with new food and bedding. The worms will sensibly head over to the fresh side after a day or two, and you can collect up the old half.

3) If the idea of physical contact with worms is just too much for you, try this no-touch trick. Drill or punch holes in the bottom of a new box, and place it over the first one. Fill it with new food and bedding, and the worms will gradually migrate up to their new home.

Dave says: 'Tiger worms are happiest at temperatures of about 8–28°C. Any colder than that, they may slow down their eating and breeding, and if they get too hot they won't survive. Make sure you keep your worms in a cool, dark spot.'

TIP: Each time you harvest the castings (known as vermicast), also check the bottom box. There should be enough fluid gathered there to make a highly potent liquid fertiliser. Dilute this fluid with water (one part worm wee to ten parts water) and use it to water your plants – they'll love it.

TIP: Don't be alarmed if you wake up to escaping worms in the first week or so! Often a few brave individuals stage an initial mad dash for freedom, but they'll settle down once they get used to their new home. They also like to crawl underneath the box or the rims of the lid so check those areas now and then.

Chooks in Town

Phil and Sarah live in a small house in the city suburbs, where they're happily raising two young boys and three healthy chickens — Maud, Edith and Lorna (in that pecking order). At the moment the chooks are each laying an egg a day, keeping the family in good supply. It's about as free range as you can get, and the satisfaction of picking up a warm egg from your backyard nest box is a pleasure no longer relegated to Nana's day. Chickens are making a comeback.

Sarah's family had always been keen on pets, but while growing up Phil had only a goldfish for company — so it has been a whole new journey for him. They reckon it's well worth it. Now that their set-up is sorted, they find the chickens pretty low maintenance, and three-year-old Otis loves collecting eggs and watching (aka chasing) the chooks. They own a cat, but the hens have the upper hand, and so far there has been no arriving outside to a silent yard and telltale pile of feathers.

own your own

1) Check the rules. If you're thinking of owning chooks, the first thing to do is check your local council's bylaws. Roosters are often out of bounds to avoid irate neighbours at 4 a.m. crow time, but usually — provided you've got something of a garden to put them in — chickens are fair play.

2) Get a coop. Readymade and kitset coops of varying types and budgets can easily be ordered online. However if you're handy with a hammer and nails, or you just like to do things the hard way, you can always build your own. A basic coop can be any shape or size, as long as there's plenty of room for your chooks to move about. It doesn't necessarily need a roof — it can be as simple as a few posts and some chicken wire. Many backyard chicken owners like to work their coop around an existing tree, which the hens will sometimes roost in. A popular coop design is an A-frame 'chicken tractor', which can be lifted and moved around the garden. This allows the chooks to scratch and fertilise different areas — great for your garden — and also provides a wire floor so that rodents, dogs and other would-be chicken thieves can't dig underneath.

3) Establish your nesting boxes. Whichever type of coop you end up with, you will need nesting boxes — preferably one box per chook. Readymade and kitset coops will have their own boxes incorporated. If you're creating your own coop you can build a simple wooden nesting box, or use recycled materials. Basically the chickens need a contained space which they can nestle into and access easily. An old wooden crate or a plastic tub with the front cut out will do the trick. Another idea of Phil and Sarah's is to use the grass-catching compartment from an old lawnmower. Whatever you use, line it with bedding such as straw or pine needles which your hens can snuggle up on. Refresh this bedding from time to time.

4) Buy your chooks. There are many different breeds, so have a think about which kind you want. If getting eggs is your primary motivation, bear in mind that some breeds are better than others for laying. Ask around, or head online to find a local supplier of your chosen

TIP: Ideally, choose a spot for your coop that's level, dry and sheltered.

breed. You can also liberate battery hens by buying directly from a battery farm or an animal shelter that's re-homing them. That way you get the double advantage of warm fuzzies from saving a life and a hen that's bred to lay.

Phil and Sarah say: 'Three is a good number of chickens to start with — enough to produce some eggs, but not too many to handle.'

5) Let 'em loose! Hens need a good coop and nesting area for overnight safety and security, but during the day they'll be quite happy clucking around the garden looking for things to entertain themselves with, such as insects, worms, grass and weeds. It's a good idea to protect seedlings, but they won't usually wreak havoc in a garden. They're big fans of grass, and will generally hang around the lawn and mow it for you. It's a good

idea to have a door or gate in your coop so that chickens can come in and out during the day, and be locked away for their own safety at night.

6) To clip or not to clip? It's not often you see a chicken soar over you. They're not big fliers, and even with unclipped wings will not usually venture further than the lower branches of a tree, or the odd visit next door. Depending on your local bylaws, and what lurks beyond your fence, it may not be necessary to have chickens with clipped wings. From the chickens' point of view, this must be a good thing.

Phil and Sarah say: 'In all the years we've owned chickens, we've only had to hop over the fence a couple of times to gather a wanderer! Our chickens never have clipped wings.'

7) Feeding your brood. Like worms, chickens are excellent little composters. They'll eat a wide variety of food scraps, including meat (yes, even chicken!) and produce fantastic natural fertiliser. If you don't have a moveable coop, get in there and scoop the poop now and then and spread it around your garden. Plants love it, and regular scooping helps keep the coop clean. Chickens also need a staple diet of grain, if you have it, or pelleted chicken feed. Do a little research in your local area to find out where to get feed. A thirty-kilogram bag will last about six weeks with three chooks.

To keep laying eggs with good shells, hens need extra calcium. They can get calcium from crushed egg shells — make sure you crush them well and mix them in with their food, so they don't cotton on to the idea of breaking eggs. Put the feed in troughs, or just scatter the food on the ground.

8) Laying, or not… Chickens are not machines, and they will have periods where they 'go off the lay'. This affects some breeds more than others, but they all have the capacity for it — and it's good to factor this into your expectations before embarking on the brave new world of chicken-raising. If one (or more) of your chooks starts spending all her time in a nesting box then she's clucky, and you won't see an egg for a while. Laying is unpredictable, but often slows down over winter — especially with older chickens. Most breeds do their best laying in their first two or three years.

Phil and Sarah say: 'When our first lot of chickens got broody, we brought them some fertilised eggs to hatch. We're not convinced it helped the laying problem, but we did enjoy watching the chicks hatch and grow up! One of our current chickens hatched out of that batch.'

9) Grim reaping. If you own chickens, there will more than likely come a time when one of them needs to go. You could give it to a 'farm' and think no more of it, get a friend to do the deed, or take a deep breath and do it yourself. The most humane way to do this is to tuck the

chook gently under one arm, in the evening, and take it away from the coop. Place a blanket over its head, which will keep it calm, and break its neck in a swift, decisive motion. Be sure you're going to go through with this before you take it on, or it will be traumatic for everyone including the chicken. Don't panic if the chicken continues moving or flapping afterwards — this is a normal reaction of their nervous system and won't last long. Phil and Sarah hadn't imagined doing this, but when the eggs hatched that they'd gifted to their broody hens they ended up with several roosters that couldn't be kept. Phil was designated the task, and while some found homes, one made a lovely coq au vin.

10) Pluck your chicken. Once the chicken has departed this world, hang it by its feet in a cool place for two to three hours. The plucking process is tedious but actually quite easy, and needn't take forever. When you

are ready to pluck, submerge the chicken in a bucket of hot water for one minute. The water should be too hot for your hand, but not boiling. Pull the chook out, and begin to pluck the larger feathers on the wings. Move on to the legs and breast. The hot water releases the feathers so they come out much more easily.

11) Dress your chicken. There are many ways to dress, or gut, a chicken — and none of them is pretty. Those of us who live in cities have got a bit prissy in recent decades. Many of our grandmothers or great-grandmothers would have gutted regularly in the days before chicken came in neatly cling-filmed supermarket packages! Use a sharp knife to remove the head at the neck, as close to the body as possible. Poke your fingers into the hole you've just created (use a rubber glove if you're squeamish) and loosen everything up a little. Turn the chicken up the other way, cut around the gap between the legs and pull out all the internal bits. It's no fun, but if you take your time it will gradually come out. Throw away the guts, unless you're brave and want to use the liver and gizzards for stock. Rinse the chicken inside and out with cold water, and cook the same day. Wash your hands and working surface thoroughly.

CHAPTER TWO

Yes-you-can
Vege Garden

No-stress Gardening with Ian

Ian Smith has been known to keep a pair of secateurs in his car, in case he drives past any delicious-looking plants hanging temptingly over people's fences. He can grow almost anything from a tiny cutting, and despite feeding his family and others with home-grown veges for decades, he rarely needs to visit a garden store.

His own father was also a keen gardener, but Ian's passion began back in the day when agricultural clubs were a part of early school life. He remembers that the rural kids would raise a calf or lamb for competition, and town kids — like Ian — grew veges.

'If you kept a gardening diary you could get an 'A' certificate. If you didn't, it was a 'B' or 'C' version,' Ian recalls. He admits he usually fell into the latter category, but he has more than made up for it with grown-up certificates in horticulture.

start a vege garden

1) 'It's in the Bag' — create the simplest garden ever!
If you're challenged when it comes to space, time and/
or patience, this is the garden for you.

- Buy four good-sized bags of organic compost.
Not too pricey, not much effort — so far so good!
- Buy or acquire seeds or seedlings that you want
to plant.
- Lie the bags flat on their sides, and make small
holes in them an equal distance apart. Ian suggests
about six holes per bag if you want to grow silverbeet
or spinach, three for tomatoes or cucumbers, and
eight or more for lettuces, etc.
- Plant seeds or seedlings directly into the holes in
the bags.
- Feed a hose or insert a watering can spout into the
bag via an additional hole to water gently.
- Voilà — an instant low-maintenance garden!

TIP: Root veges (ones that grow under-
ground) such as potatoes and pumpkin are
not good choices for this easy garden
method, as they won't have enough depth
to grow properly.

2) Alternatively, try the tyre rotation system.
If you're just starting out or don't have much space,
never fear — you can still have a highly productive
vege garden. Here's how…

- Get a bunch of used tyres from a car shop or garage.
- If you have a small patch of garden, place the tyres
on it — start by making stacks of two tyres each, and
line the bottoms with cardboard from old boxes or
cartons. (Avoid anything with lots of printing on it,
as the ink will leach into your soil.)

TIP: A pane of glass, such as an old shower
door, can be placed over the tyres. This will
act as a cloche or greenhouse when you are
establishing young seedlings. Angle the glass
or rest it on blocks to allow air to circulate.

- If you have no garden, you can still use this method
on a deck or balcony. Place some plastic underneath
the tyres to protect your surface — or use pots
instead.
- For a good fertile soil, fill the tyres with some damp,
shredded newspaper as a base layer; manure if you
can get some (see p. 13); wet hay or grass clippings if
you have them; and soil or potting mix on top.
- Plant a different vege in each tyre stack, being
aware that different types of veges require different
amounts of space. Check the 'Seasonal Planting
Diary' (p. 34) to see which seedlings suit the time of
year.

Ian says: 'The beauty of the tyre system
is that it's easy to give each plant what it
needs without affecting those around it,
which may have different requirements.
A bit like kids with their own bedroom!'

- As each plant finishes its season, don't replace it
with seedlings of the same vege, but instead choose
another one. Rotate your plants from tyre to tyre
each year.

Ian says: 'Planting the same plants in the
same place each year means the same
nutrients are sucked out of the soil, and the
same diseases build up. Rotating your
plants stops this from happening.'

TIP: When you replace a tyre, you're actually paying the tyre store to get rid of your old one too — it's usually built into the price. So if someone asks them for used tyres, they'll 'generously' give them away. Bingo! It's a win-win.

basic anaerobic compost

Ian is the fount of all knowledge when it comes to saving both time and money. Here's the most simple version of compost you'll ever come across — if you lack space or energy but have plenty of patience, this one's for you!

1) Put a bunch of any compostable scraps — vege peelings, grass clippings, leaves, etc. — into a plastic supermarket bag.

2) Throw in some soil.

3) Dampen it all with a little water (not too much).

4) Squeeze excess air out of the bag, and tie it; repeat the process for as many bags as you wish.

5) Put the bags down the end of your garden.

6) Leave for eighteen months.

7) You now have compost!

· If you have lots of garden space, all the same principles apply for raised or in-ground vege beds — just on a grander scale.

Ian says: 'You don't need to be too fussy about rows or exact distances between plants. They don't know maths — plant them in any pattern, and they'll still grow!'

28

TIP: The organisms that break down anaerobic compost are the type that usually live in dark, swampy places where humans dare not tread. They release gases that smell nasty. If you're using this method, keep the bags away from the house and protect them from pets and pests. If you don't like the sound of this, go for Sister Loyola's sweet-smelling alternative! (See 'Sister Loyola's Compost', p. 12.)

garden tips and tricks

Sister Loyola says she felt 'like a stunned mullet' when she won a top gardening award, and Ian Smith claims he's 'no expert or anything'. But between them, they have over a century of highly successful gardening experience, and have picked up many a cost-cutting and bug-busting tip along the way. Here are a few of the best that will keep you growing happy little veges (whilst maintaining a happy little wallet, and a happy little planet).

1) Cooking with eggs? Save the shells and crumble them around your growing vegetables to stop slugs and snails getting to them. How does it work? Well, if your body were that squishy, you'd stay away from sharp edges too! Ideally, dry the shells first by leaving them in a low oven for a bit — this hardens them and creates a snail version of razor wire.

2) Coffee grounds are a gardener's best friend. Next time you make a coffee, instead of throwing the grounds down the sink (you shouldn't do that anyway — what were you thinking?), put them aside for the vege patch. Dig the grounds into the soil — they are excellent as a slow-release nitrogen source; add them to the compost as 'green' matter (for compost purposes they're green, trust me); or feed them to the worms in your worm farm. Worms are caffeine fiends and love a good espresso now and then. Just make sure you put all the grounds in one spot instead of sprinkling them around so the worms can ration themselves. If you're feeling more adventurous (and patient), you can even brew a coffee 'tea'. Put a cup or two of coffee grounds into an old sock, tie it up well and leave it in a bucket of water for a fortnight. The result is a fabulous liquid fertiliser for sprinkling or spraying over plants. Slugs and snails aren't fans of coffee, so the grounds also make a good pest deterrent. Shake some alongside your egg shells to repel would-be invaders.

TIP: Cafés collect their discarded grounds, and are usually more than happy to get rid of them. Offer to take the grounds off their hands. Sister Loyola regularly heads down to a local café in the ute and picks up bag loads for the Home of Compassion garden.

4) Pine needles are another great defence against squishy-bodied pests. Lay them on garden paths and between beds, but not on the garden itself as they're too acidic for veges.

5) Vege gardens can be pretty too, and the right flowers are friends with benefits. Blue flowers are irresistible to wandering bees, and marigolds look beautiful while also scaring pests away. Calendula, planted in your favourite patio pot, will stop your dog peeing on the pot, and is also an ingredient in a great homemade skin cream (see p. 114). Chamomile looks lovely and is known as the 'plant doctor'. It will perk up any struggling veges if planted beside them, and when it flowers you can make a relaxing tea by soaking the petals in cold water overnight (see p. 83).

3) Artemesia (aka wormwood) and comfrey are two plants that Sister Loyola suggests every garden needs. Artemesia is an excellent pest-repellent, and is great to plant at the edges of beds if you have a reasonable garden space. The foliage can also be scattered around your plants to ward off unwanted vege-munchers. Tarragon is a type of artemesia and a brilliant herb for cooking too — so it's win-win! Comfrey is easy to grow, seeds itself, and is a wonderful natural fertiliser. Sister Loyola makes a comfrey 'tea' by soaking a stocking-full in water (as per the coffee version). This is also said to heal sprains, so if you fall down a bank while planting comfrey, make sure you grab enough leaves on the way to make a compress…

waste not, want not

Ian Smith is not one to pass up an opportunity for free plants, and he has cultivated many a bountiful vegetable crop as a result of discarded peelings or a quick snip of the secateurs. If you're keen to reduce your trips to the garden centre, and make use of what you already have, here's how.

1) Plant seeds. Many veges contain seeds within themselves that can be dried and germinated for planting. Collect that puddle of tomato seeds left behind on your chopping board, for example, or the pumpkin seeds you just scraped out. Experiment with planting these seeds to generate a new plant.
- *Tomatoes*: Dry the seeds for a few days on a piece of tissue, then plant. According to Ian, tomatoes are the easiest seeds to germinate in this way. Note that you may not always end up with the same type of tomato that the seeds came from, because of crossbreeding (e.g. cherry tomato seeds may grow a full-sized tomato plant and vice versa).
- *Beans*: Dry the pods. Once dry, split the pods open and plant the seeds.
- *Pumpkin*: Wash the seeds, then leave to dry before planting (as for tomatoes).

2) Use leftovers. Before you throw out your ageing veges, consider whether they're worth planting.
- Garlic cloves can be separated and planted, and will sprout naturally. Plant them a fair way into your soil, ideally in winter. If the weather is warm, leave them in the fridge for a week first. Garlic's not that smart and will think it is winter after all.
- Sprout potatoes from bought ones by exposing them to the light a good two months before you plan to plant. You should see strong sprouts appearing.

TIP: Aspirin was originally made by boiling up willow bark. Although it's now made synthetically, the active ingredient has similar properties and can give your cutting a boost. Dissolve one aspirin in water and soak the stem base before planting.

TIP: Save toilet rolls to use as seedling planters. Place several inside an empty plastic container, fill each with soil or potting mix and plant your seeds. Once your seedlings are ready for the garden, you can plant the whole toilet roll — it will break down naturally in the soil. This technique is great for reducing transplant shock, recycles, and is much cheaper than expensive peat pots.

Aim for short, thick sprouts, not the spindly, white tentacles you get from leaving potatoes in the cupboard too long. Ian even sprouts potatoes and kumara from chopped ends and thick peelings. If you're trying this, put the ends in a container with a little water and expose them to light for two to three months.

3) Collect cuttings. Some plants grow better than others from cuttings, but Ian reckons it's always worth giving it a go. He's had plenty of success with cuttings he didn't expect to survive, and also occasional failures with plants that are supposed to take well. Using cuttings does involve a bit of trial and error, but for limited effort you might just get yourself a free plant.

• Choose a healthy looking 'mother plant' from which to take your cutting. Ask permission to take a cutting if it's not on your property — no sneaking over the neighbour's fence or balcony at night!

• Pick a green stem towards the edges of the mother plant, with newer growth on it.

• Count back two sets of leaves from the tip of the stem, and cut neatly, just above the join of the second set. You should now have a nice little stem with two or three leaves on it — this is your cutting.

• Plant the base of the stem in some water or good compost or potting mix, and keep it in a moist, warm indoor environment — like a windowsill. You can place a clear plastic bag over the cutting to help keep up the moisture levels.

• If you want to give your cutting a helping hand, you could buy a growth hormone from the garden store that will stimulate root growth. Alternatively, if there are willows nearby, shave the bark from the twigs of a willow tree. Soak the bark and your stem base in water for a natural root stimulant.

Seasonal Planting Diary

The Seasonal Planting Diary is a rough calendar indicating when to plant what, with a list of simple and easily accessible veges. Use it as a guide only, adjusting the diary to suit the climate in which you live and your gardening circumstances. If winter is lingering on, for example, and your balcony or garden patch won't see the sun for another month, hold off planting those spring veges. Likewise, if you live somewhere that stays pretty warm all year round, try planting some extra summer veges in the winter months.

Get to know these basic plants, and their requirements, for a season or three. If it's going well, branch out and try some others, such as peppers, pumpkins and eggplants.

Season	Seeds to get started	Plant out in garden or pots	Rewards to be reaped!	To-do list
Early spring	Lettuces, Zucchini, Tomatoes	Carrots, Lettuces, Onions, Early potatoes, Garlic	Silverbeet, Brassicas (cabbages, cauliflowers, broccoli, bok choy, brussels sprouts, etc.), Leeks	Blossom has started, which is great motivation to get some seeds going. Give garden or pots a dose of compost anywhere you've removed crops.
Mid spring	Green beans, Carrots, Zucchini, Lettuces, Silverbeet, Beetroot	Carrots, Lettuces, Early potatoes, Silverbeet	Silverbeet, Brassicas, Leeks	You'll be busy! It's all about planting this month, but hold off if the weather's still cold and/or wet. It won't be long.
Late spring	Green beans, Carrots, Lettuces, Beetroot	Green beans, Tomatoes, Carrots, Zucchini, Lettuces, Potatoes, Silverbeet, Beetroot	Silverbeet, Broad beans, Broccoli, Onions	Get out into that garden or onto that balcony and plant, plant, plant. Check your veges have enough water if things are warm and/or windy.
Early summer	Carrots, Lettuces, Green beans	Green beans, Leeks, Carrots, Zucchini, Lettuces, Potatoes, Silverbeet, Beetroot	Broad beans, Carrots, Lettuces, Onions, Early potatoes, Silverbeet	Your plants will most likely be getting thirsty and weeds will be growing quickly, so stay on top of your watering and weeding. The good news is that there'll be plenty to pick.

Mid summer	Brassicas, Lettuces	Green beans, Carrots, Lettuces, Leeks, Beetroot	Green beans, Carrots, Zucchini, Garlic, Lettuces, Early potatoes, Silverbeet, Tomatoes	Keep up the maintenance, and get busy in the kitchen! With all that bounty there'll be some preserving to do…
Late summer	Brassicas, Green beans, Lettuces	Carrots, Lettuces, Brassicas	Green beans, Carrots, Zucchini, Lettuces, Last of the early potatoes, Silverbeet, Tomatoes, Onions	Watering and weeding as for mid summer. You'll be inundated with tomatoes about now, if you planted them on time, so check out Grisham's recipes on p. 46.
Early autumn	Brassicas	Lettuces, Green beans, Brassicas	Carrots, Zucchini, Lettuces, Potatoes, Silverbeet, Tomatoes	Autumn is an excellent season for compost. Rake up those leaves as they start to fall and add them to your compost pile. Harvest regularly to keep your veges producing.
Mid autumn	Brassicas, Broad beans	Brassicas	Green beans, Carrots, Zucchini, Lettuces, Potatoes, Silverbeet, Tomatoes, Brassicas	Pull out any annual plants that have finished their run, or let them go to seed and collect the seeds for next year. Dry the seeds, and store in airtight containers. Keep raking up those leaves!
Late autumn	Broad beans	Broad beans, Brassicas, Garlic	Lettuces, Carrots, Potatoes, Brassicas, Silverbeet	Put your soil to bed for winter under a duvet of mulch. Mulches can be bought at garden stores, or else cover soil with a layer of wood chips, tree bark, dried leaves, pine needles, straw, etc.
Early winter	Brassicas	Broad beans, Garlic	Brassicas, Carrots, Silverbeet	Even if you don't like broad beans, plant some — they'll keep the soil in good shape over winter. Start to plan what you want to plant where next year. Remember not to plant the same crops in the same place!
Mid winter	Brassicas	Broad beans, Garlic (traditionally, garlic is planted on the shortest day of the year)	Brassicas, Carrots, Leeks, Silverbeet	Keep your compost pile ticking over with a fresh hit of seaweed or manure, and apply compost to any newly vacant areas.
Late winter	Tomatoes, Lettuces, Carrots	Garlic, Onions, Early potatoes	Leeks, Silverbeet, Brassicas	Time to up the momentum with those seed trays — spring is a-comin'! Put compost anywhere plants have been removed.

The Three Must-grows

Your cupboards need never be bare if you have a crop each of:

- tomatoes
- lemons
- potatoes.

tomatoes in the fast lane

Tomatoes are easy to grow and particularly prolific. They'll grow in just about any soil, and are an excellent choice for impatient people, as they change so fast during summer you can almost *see* them grow! Tomatoes can be grown equally well in pots or gardens, indoors or outdoors. If you're new to the whole gardening thing and want to give just one plant a go, make it a tomato.

1) Before you embark on planting, decide which type of tomato you want. There are many different shapes, sizes and varieties, and some may suit your climate better than others.

2) Tomatoes grow well from seeds and cuttings. Get them started in seed trays, about a month before you plan to plant them outside. They don't mind being transplanted but get pushy with close neighbours, so move them into larger pots once they get their first leaves. They are space hogs and need plenty of room to spread out.

3) Usually tomatoes are planted outside in mid spring. Their main requirements are good sun and three months of frost-free growing time in warm soil. Depending on where you live, this could mean anytime between late winter and early summer. Plant them about a metre apart from each other — they grow like wild fire when they get going. Keep them upright by tying them gently to a stake with garden twine or old pantyhose or tights.

4) Planting in tyres (p. 27) is effective for tomatoes — it gives them plenty of space to themselves, and the black tyres retain the heat from the sun. There's nothing a tomato likes better than warm feet! If you're planting them in pots, move them around when you can to follow the sun.

5) Like lemons, tomatoes need plenty of water to reach down to their roots. Try the cut-off bottle technique (see tip, p. 38) to get the water where it needs to go. Pull back on the watering a little once the fruit begins to ripen, so it stays sweet — but don't let the plant dry out.

6) Pick your tomatoes as soon as they are fully ripe. They'll quickly go mushy if you leave them (if the birds haven't flown in for the feast by then). If you suddenly find you're inundated with ripe tomatoes, it's time to get into the kitchen and give Grisham's recipes a go! (See p. 46.)

7) Once the plant has finished fruiting, pull out the whole plant and dig compost into the spot it used to fill. To avoid your tomatoes developing diseases, don't plant them or their potato cousins in the same place next year.

TIP: Potatoes and tomatoes are from the same family, and susceptible to the same diseases. Don't plant your potatoes where you have recently been growing tomatoes.

TIP: Cut the bottom off a plastic milk or soft drink bottle and plant it about half a metre from your lemon tree (or at the edge of the pot) with the top protruding. Once a week, take the lid off the bottle and pour some water into it. This will give the roots a good soak.

lemons are a winner

It's hard to find a reason not to plant lemon trees. They're bright, prolific and easy to grow, plus they produce fruit that can be used in almost any recipe — from marinades to marmalades. They're also a staple ingredient in many homemade cleaning products (see p. 107). Fresh lemons were a favourite of our grandparents' generation — back in the days before lemon juice came in squeezy bottles — and they're making a strong comeback. Lemon trees don't mind being contained in a decent-sized pot, so they make a great home-grown fruit even if you only have indoor or patio space.

1) If planting outdoors, plant your baby lemon seedling in early autumn or spring to give it the best possible start in life.

2) Lemons love the sun, so pick the sunniest position you can find. If you're growing your lemon tree in a pot, you can move it around to sunbathe. Pot or container planting is also a good idea if you live in a climate that gets frosty, as you can bring your lemon tree indoors during the winter months. They're not so keen on freezing.

3) Water your lemon tree well once a week, rather than a little bit every day. Lemons love a good long drink but don't like wet pants — make sure the soil drains well!

good ol' spuds

According to my own Nana, 'Everything goes with potatoes.' The humble potato is a staple the world over, and reputedly kept the Irish alive for years. A decent potato crop can keep your food bill down, and will give you the satisfaction of harvesting home-grown food with very little effort on your part. In fact, my Dad reckons the best way to grow potatoes is accidentally — by leaving some bought ones in the bag for too long, then chucking the sprouting mess into the garden. We did once grow surprise potatoes that way, but I'd recommend Ian Smith's method for a greater chance of success:

1) Used tyres are excellent for growing potatoes. Whether or not you're planting other veges in tyres, get down to your local tyre store and pick up a few for the potatoes.

2) Establish your soil as per Ian Smith's yes-you-can vege garden (p. 27).

3) Buy some seed potatoes, or sprout your own from a variety that you like (see p. 32).

Ian says: 'When I was growing up people just ate potatoes. Now there are all kinds of fancy names for different sorts!'

4) Expose the seed potatoes or peelings to the light for a month or two before planting, to allow thick shoots to form (avoid direct sunlight).

5) Plant your sprouted potato about ten centimetres down into the soil. You can fit three potato plants in a standard tyre — space them evenly apart.

6) As the sprout grows, the leafy part of the potato plant will appear above ground. When it gets to about ten to fifteen centimetres above the soil level, gently place another tyre on top of the existing one and build the soil up around the plant. Be careful to leave some of the plant above ground — the leaves need to find the light.

7) Keep building this way (adding more tyres if necessary) until the plant flowers. Take care not to let the plant grow too high without building, or your baby potatoes will be exposed to the light and will turn green.

8) When the plant has finished flowering, your potatoes are ready! Dig down to harvest.

Ian says: 'Green potatoes and potato sprouts are poisonous — they won't do huge harm in small amounts, but they will definitely give you a bellyache.'

CHAPTER THREE

From the Garden

Love Your Lemons

Whether you've grown your own, nicked some from over the neighbour's fence or picked up a big bag at the market, here are some ideas if you should find yourself with an excess of lemons…

old-fashioned lemonade

The thought of homemade lemonade can make many an older person all misty-eyed and nostalgic. The traditional recipe is simple and refreshing. Make it nana-style for a perfect summer treat!

INGREDIENTS

1 cup sugar
1 cup water
1 cup lemon juice
3-4 cups extra water (approx.)
ice and wedges of lemon, to serve

1) Combine the sugar and water in a saucepan. Stir gently over a low heat until all the sugar has dissolved.

2) Pour the mixture into a large jug, and stir in the lemon juice. Top up with the extra water until it tastes just how you like it.

3) Place in the fridge to chill. Serve with plenty of ice and wedges of lemon.

TIP: To make pink lemonade, simply replace one cup of the extra water with fresh cranberry juice.

lemon sorbet

INGREDIENTS

½ cup sugar
1 cup water
1 cup lemon juice
2-4 Tbsp grated lemon zest (optional)

1) Combine the sugar and water in a saucepan. Stir gently over a low heat until all the sugar has dissolved.

2) Pour the mixture into a large jug, stirring in the lemon juice and grated lemon zest.

3) Pour the mixture into a container and freeze for an hour or two until it is not quite solid.

4) Whisk with a fork to make the semi-frozen mixture light and fluffy.

5) Freeze until just solid, then blend in a food processor or blender until smooth.

6) Pop it back in the freezer until you want to serve it.

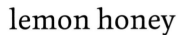

TIP: Try adding crushed berries for extra deliciousness.

lemon honey

This is an absolute favourite of Pat and Mary (see p. 61). Mary makes large batches for the church fair each year, where she says it 'sells like hot cakes'.

INGREDIENTS
100 g butter
250 g sugar
4 eggs (beaten)
juice and grated rind of 2 lemons

1) Place the butter in a heatproof bowl, and fit the bowl inside a saucepan of water. Heat the water gently to melt the butter.

Pat says: 'Adding a little lemon juice will make the butter melt more quickly.'

2) Add the sugar, beaten eggs, lemon juice and grated rind.

3) Beat briefly to combine and allow to simmer for up to 20 minutes, stirring occasionally.

Mary says: 'It will thicken like a custard. Mmmm — delicious.'

4) Pour into small prepared jars. Great for gifts (or selling at church fairs…)

salted lemons

INGREDIENTS
1 kg lemons
½ cup salt (approx.), preferably coarse

1) Prepare glass jar(s), by washing well with hot water and putting into an oven at a low temperature.

2) 'Butterfly' the lemons by nearly cutting in half lengthwise (don't cut all the way through). Gently open the lemon and — without slicing all the way through — cut in half again to create quarters.

3) Fan the lemon open, keeping the quarters attached to each other, and sprinkle all over with salt.

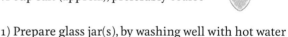

TIP: Coarse salt, like sea salt, is best for preserving lemons.

4) Remove your jar from the oven and place 2 Tbsp salt in the bottom.

5) Tightly pack the salted lemons into the jar, pushing them down to release the juice. The juice should fill the jar as you pack, covering the top of the lemons when the jar is full. If not, add more juice until the lemons are covered.

TIP: For a bit of spice, try adding whole cloves, cinnamon sticks or peppercorns to the jar.

6) Add approx. 2 Tbsp more salt, and seal the jar tightly.

7) Leave the jar to cure somewhere warm, such as the windowsill or hot water cupboard, for a few days. Turn it upside down now and then to distribute the salt evenly. (Make sure you use a leak-proof jar!)

8) Refrigerate for about a month before using, still turning occasionally.

9) Salted lemons are ideal in African or Middle Eastern-inspired cooking. If you remove each lemon with clean tongs, the jar should keep for six months to a year. Rinse lemons before eating.

Grisham's Glut of Tomatoes

When Grisham Langston was given a ten-kilogram bag of fresh tomatoes by his mother-in-law one Christmas, he knew he'd have to get creative. Luckily, he had plenty of ideas up his sleeve. An at-home father of three, Grisham knows his way around a kitchen. He too spent his toddler years at home with Dad, while his mother — a lawyer — brought home the bacon. It was something his Dad took a bit of flak for in those days. Both parents were back working full time once he started school, so Grisham and his sister were allocated a night each to cook for the family. Grisham took to it like a duck to water. His sister tried everything to wriggle out of it. Happily for them both, they reached a successful trade deal. Grisham would do both nights of cooking, if his sister did both nights of dishes!

If you're growing your own tomatoes, you'll find they're prolific little fruiters and you'll be wondering what to do with them all. Or, like Grisham, you may have ended up with a random bag load. Many kilos of tomatoes later, these recipes are Grisham's favourites — and they have been given a big thumbs-up from the kids too.

oven-dried tomatoes

INGREDIENT

tomatoes

1) 'Butterfly' the tomatoes by nearly cutting them in half (don't cut all the way through). Open them out like a book.

2) De-seed the tomatoes by scooping out the mushy stuff (optional).

Grisham says: 'If you choose not to de-seed the tomatoes, they'll take longer to dry, but will end up juicier. Your call.'

3) Pop them in the oven on a baking tray, at the lowest temperature. Leave until dry. (Bear in mind this could take all day, so make sure you have plenty of time!)

4) Check them now and then, and remove before they feel brittle. Place on a cake rack to cool.

Oven-dried Tomatoes will last several months in an airtight bag or jar.

preserved tomatoes

INGREDIENTS

Oven-dried Tomatoes (see p. 46)
chilli flakes (optional)
fresh herbs (e.g. oregano, basil)
olive oil

1) Pack your Oven-dried Tomatoes into a prepared jar (see p. 69 for jar prep).

2) Sprinkle the chilli flakes and fresh herbs over them, and cover with olive oil. Seal the jar.

Preserved Tomatoes will last up to a year and look great on display. The marinade gives the Oven-dried Tomatoes gorgeous flavour; they are excellent in antipasto.

tomato ketchup

Every kid knows stuff tastes better with tomato sauce on it! Grisham's easy recipe has less sugar than most versions, and will last up to two years in the bottle.

INGREDIENTS

3 kg tomatoes (roughly chopped)
500 g onions (roughly chopped)
200 g sugar
1 cup cider vinegar
¼ cup salt
2 Tbsp whole cloves
1 tsp cayenne pepper
2 Tbsp juniper berries (optional — can be replaced
   with 1 Tbsp allspice)

1) Put everything in a saucepan, bring to the boil and simmer for 3-4 hours.

Grisham says: "Yes, you really do have to leave it this long — so it can reduce and thicken."

2) Strain through a colander or sieve into prepared bottles. Makes 3 litres.

TIP: Grisham uses empty plastic tomato ketchup bottles, though you could also use prepared glass jars or bottles (p. 69). Prepare plastic bottles by putting them through the dishwasher, or half fill with water and microwave on high for thirty seconds to one minute.

tomato chutney

INGREDIENTS

800 g tomatoes, chopped (fresh is best, but tinned
   will work)
300 ml cider vinegar
150 g sugar
16 cloves of garlic, crushed (that should keep the
   vampires away!)
8 cm root ginger, grated
2 Tbsp raisins or sultanas
2 tsp salt
2 tsp chilli powder

1) Put everything in a saucepan, bring to the boil and
simmer for 1½-2 hours.

2) When cool, pour into prepared jars (see p. 69).
Makes a 500 ml jar of chutney.

basic pasta sauce

Make a big batch of this and freeze it in portions for
a quick pasta meal whenever you want one!

INGREDIENTS

3 Tbsp olive oil
2 onions (roughly chopped)
2 cloves garlic (crushed)
1 dozen tomatoes (approx., or 2 regular 400 g cans)
1 cup red wine (optional — can be replaced with
   water or vegetable stock)
3 Tbsp chopped herbs (e.g. basil, oregano, thyme)
salt and pepper (to taste)

1) Heat the oil in a stainless steel saucepan, add
the garlic and onion, and fry until soft.

TIP: When cooking with tomatoes, use a stainless steel pan. Cast iron and aluminium will react with the acidity of the tomatoes, giving your food a metallic taste.

2) Add the remaining ingredients and bring to the boil.

3) Simmer for half an hour, removing fresh tomato
skins with a fork or tongs as they begin to loosen.

4) Serve immediately with your favourite pasta.
Alternatively keep the sauce in the fridge for a few
days, or freeze in portions to use throughout the year.

tomato juice

INGREDIENTS

1.5 kg ripe tomatoes (cored and roughly chopped)
2 or 3 sticks celery (chopped, including leaves)
1 onion (chopped)
1 Tbsp sugar
salt and pepper (to taste)
tabasco sauce (optional — to taste)

1) Combine all ingredients in a large stainless steel
saucepan and bring to the boil. Simmer uncovered for
about half an hour.

2) Using the back of a spoon, press the mixture through
a sieve into a bowl, or put it through a food mill.

3) Allow to cool, chill and serve.

TIP: Pop in some vodka and a celery stick and you've got yourself a Bloody Mary. Add a little Worcestershire or tabasco sauce if you fancy.

green tomato salsa

If you grow your own tomatoes, they're usually still fruiting by the time you're getting keen to plant something else. Go ahead and pull them out! Use any remaining green ones to make this refreshing salsa — excellent with nachos.

INGREDIENTS
500 g green tomatoes
water
1 onion (roughly chopped)
2 cloves garlic
2 Tbsp chopped coriander
3 chillies, or 1½ tsp minced chilli (ideally jalapeno)
½ tsp sugar
salt (to taste)

1) In a saucepan, cover the green tomatoes with water, bring to the boil and simmer for about 5 minutes until tender.

2) Drain the water into a jug and set aside.

3) Put the tomatoes and remaining ingredients in a food processor or blender, and pulse briefly to combine — don't make it too smooth.

4) Add the reserved water a little at a time until you get a salsa that is chunky, yet soft enough for dipping.

Parsley

– the Wonder Herb

Bernice Gleadow grew up in the days before credit cards when 'conservation' was a survival skill. As a child, she remembers heading off on the train for home economics lessons each week, clutching a little wicker basket and a tea towel. There she learnt how to get the most out of every ingredient. Nothing was wasted, and knowing the nutritional value of everything was vital. Bernice went on to teach home economics herself, and the one food she can't speak highly enough about is parsley.

These days parsley is seen as a bit boring in a line-up of herbs, and is often relegated to the role of garnish. But it is an excellent antioxidant, a good source of folic acid, and is high in Vitamin C — making it a great replacement for citrus fruits in the winter months when they can get expensive. In short, parsley is something of a wonder herb. Better yet, it's cheap to buy and easy to grow!

growing parsley

There are two main types of parsley: curly and flat leaf. You'll most often see the curly leaf version garnishing food, whereas the flat leaf variety has a stronger flavour so is usually preferred for cooking. In the end it's your call — straight or curly…?

Parsley is a fairly hardy little plant that grows well in pots, so it's great for apartment-dwellers and people on the move. Ordinary soil or potting mix will suit parsley just fine — it's pretty forgiving, and grows like a weed in some areas.

Bernice says, 'Just stick it in the ground,

water it and it'll grow!'

If you're planting parsley from seeds, be patient: it can take up to a month to germinate. The seeds like warm soil, so plant in summer or indoors. Let your seedling grow to a good twenty centimetres or so before transplanting it into the garden.

Personally I'm not so big on patience, so I opt for parsley seedlings. Many supermarkets sell parsley in small pots in the herb section. These plants can

easily be transplanted into your garden or a bigger indoor pot for a permanent parsley supply. If you're also growing tomatoes or roses, parsley is the perfect companion! Plant the parsley nearby to repel pests naturally. Luckily, the one bug that does like parsley is the bee, which is another bonus for your garden.

Parsley is relaxed about a cooler climate, and doesn't need loads of sun to

TIP: To fast-track the process, soak the seeds in water overnight and pour boiling hot water on the soil before planting.

TIP: Allow your parsley to flower and go to seed — it will self-sow and grow baby parsleys for next season.

eating parsley

Pick the outer leaves from your parsley plant. You can wash these leaves and eat them fresh; lay them out to dry and crumble them into a container for storage; or use them fresh in cooking and garnishes.

There are countless recipes that use parsley, but one of Bernice's favourites is a simple Middle Eastern tabouleh. She's kept her children and grandchildren healthy with it for years.

simple tabouleh

INGREDIENTS

⅔ cup bulgur wheat or couscous (optional)

1½ cups chopped parsley (ideally flat leaf, but curly
    is fine too)

handful chopped mint leaves

2 spring onions

2 tomatoes

juice of 1 lemon

2-3 Tbsp olive oil

salt and pepper (to taste)

1) If using bulgur wheat, soak in water for 2-3 hours,
then drain off excess water. If using couscous, place in a
bowl with an equal quantity of boiling water (or stock),
cover, and leave to stand for about 5 minutes.

TIP: Traditional tabouleh uses less
bulgur wheat or couscous than western
versions, or even none at all. For a
good fresh parsley feast, leave it out
altogether!

2) Combine all ingredients in a bowl, mix and serve.

Tabouleh makes an excellent filling for pita bread or
accompaniment for kebabs, and is delicious on its
own as a salad. If you want to get fancy, eat it using a
scooped leaf from an iceberg lettuce.

TIP: Just eaten onions and been caught
without your toothbrush? Parsley is
excellent for freshening the breath,
and also helps with indigestion.

Connie's Marmalade

My own Nana and her supreme marmalade-making abilities inspired this book. So famous is Nana's marmalade that she maintains a constant stash 'cellared' under her bed to meet family demand. What I didn't know until recently, was that Nana learned to make marmalade as a child in the 1920s from her own mother — my Great-Nana, Florence Butler. Florence's marmalade was so delicious that Nana claims she would have eaten it 'morning, noon and night' if she'd had the chance. She admits she's still prone to reach under her bed for a jar before lights-out...

Nana's marmalade

INGREDIENTS

1 grapefruit
2 oranges
3 cups water
juice of 1 lemon
1 kg sugar

1) Grate the zest from the grapefruit and oranges, and set aside.

2) Cut the fruit in half, and squeeze the juice into a large bowl.

nana says: 'make sure you get the pips in there too — don't throw them out! Pips contain pectin, which will help the marmalade to gel.'

3) Cut the flesh into pieces.

4) Blend the flesh in a food processor or blender with a little of the water.

5) Add the blended pulp to the bowl of juice, along with the remaining water, the zest and the lemon juice.

TIP: Nana suggests splitting the quantity of chopped fruit into two halves and blending separately, to be kind to your blender. Depends on your blender really! If you bought it from a garage sale, best listen to Nana.

6) Cover, and leave to sit overnight.

7) The next day, bring it to the boil in a saucepan. Simmer until the fruit is very soft.

8) Stir in the sugar. Simmer for a further 45 minutes, and test for setting.

9) When set, pour the marmalade into prepared jars (see p. 69).

10) Makes an impressive 4-5 jars of marmalade, which should keep well in a cool cupboard for several months.

TIP: To test for setting, put a little of the marmalade on a teaspoon and place it in the freezer for a minute or two to cool. Test the marmalade by pulling your finger gently through the sample. If it wrinkles, it's ready. If not, boil the marmalade for a little longer before testing again.

under pressure

A quicker way of boiling marmalade is in a pressure cooker. That's what Nana likes to do these days. Pressure cookers (aka pressure canners or retorts) are large sealed pots that allow cooking at higher temperatures. They're relatively easy to come by and a worthwhile investment if you think you might get into marmalades, jams or home-canning of any type. If you're using a pressure cooker, follow these steps instead, once the fruit and juices have sat overnight:

- The next day, tip the mixture into a pressure cooker and cook at full steam for 10-15 minutes.
- Let the steam slowly subside until 'the knobby thing is ready', as per the instructions on your cooker. (Nana likes to do a crossword while she's waiting, but I'll leave you to find your own fun activity...)
- Remove the lid, and add the sugar.
- Cook (uncovered) on a low heat, stirring carefully until all the sugar has completely dissolved.
- Bring to a steady boil.

nana says: 'Keep stirring occasionally to remind it you're in charge.'

- After about twenty minutes, do a set test (see p. 56). When set, pour the marmalade into prepared jars (see p. 69).

TIP: Pressure cookers are so named for a reason: the vacuum seal allows significant pressure to build up inside. Read your cooker's manual carefully, and be patient! Don't be tempted to open the lid before the steam has properly subsided or you could have a hot marmalade explosion to deal with. Nana exploded her marmalade all over her pension flat a couple of years ago, and though she did her best with a mop, Nana's really not that tall — you can still find plenty of orange specks on her ceiling.

TIP: If you're lacking in time or apartment space, try using the same ingredients with the microwave cooking instructions for 'Easy Jam' (p. 59). The marmalade won't set as firmly, but it will still taste good. Just don't tell Nana.

Born to a single mother in the middle of the Depression, John's start to life was far from easy. He remembers getting up to all sorts of mischief as a small boy, before being sent off to a convent to be 'ironed out' by the nuns. Ironing (almost) complete, he was taken in by a family as a boarder when he hit his teens. The father of the family was an excellent jam-maker, and taught young John the tricks of the trade. Over the years John developed a few tricks of his own, and now, at nearly eighty, he has adapted the recipe to suit his tiny retirement studio. His recipe is ideal for those short on space or time, and is amazingly straightforward.

easy jam

This recipe will work with pretty much any type of fruit you fancy. Get creative with combos!

INGREDIENTS
2 cups chopped fruit
2 cups sugar
1 whole chopped lemon

1) Wash the fruit, and place it in a microwave-safe bowl or large jug. If you're using a fruit with skin, such as tamarillos or kiwifruit, simply cut off the tops and put in whole — use about 1 dozen.

2) Add enough water to just cover the fruit.

3) Microwave on high for about 7 minutes (adjust timing if necessary to suit your microwave).

TIP: If you don't have a microwave, or prefer to cook on the stove, use the same ingredients with the boiling instructions from 'Nana's Marmalade' (p. 55). Peel fruit before cooking.

4) Drain the water. If you have used whole, thicker-skinned fruit, peel the skin off — it should now come away easily without any waste.

5) Use a potato masher to mash the fruit.

John says: 'Just belt all hell out of it!'

6) Stir in the sugar and the lemon.

7) Microwave on high for another 7 minutes, then test to see if the jam is set.

8) Pour into prepared jars (see p. 69), seal the jars, and stick on a personalised label!

TIP: Old-fashioned jam doesn't need any special setting ingredients. Instead it relies on the natural pectin in fruit to set to a soft, smooth texture — yum! If you do like more bounce in your jam, simply stir in a tablespoonful of gelatine before the final cooking.

TIP: To test if your jam is set, Nana suggests putting a little on a teaspoon, and placing in the freezer for a minute or two to cool. Pull it out and poke it — if it wrinkles, it's set. If not, cook for a little longer, but keep testing at regular intervals.

TIP: It's a good idea to cover the bowl or jug when cooking, or you'll spend the next few hours scraping sticky jam out of the microwave's every crevice. I learnt this the hard way.

Pickles
and
Preserves
with
Pat
and
Mary

Pat Philips and Mary Allan have been friends for over fifty years. They were both wives of army officers, and first met on a ship which was carrying both families to a new station in post-war Malaysia. Now widowed, they live only a few doors away from each other, and are prolific makers of almost anything that comes in a jar. Pat makes beautifully presented preserves for the Save the Children shop, and local fairs never need worry about running out of treats and treasures with Mary around. Children during the Depression, both women credit their own mothers for the skills they have inherited. Despite supplies being so scarce, they remember there was — somehow — always food on the table.

basic chutney

Pat has tried making almost every kind of chutney over the years, and keeps her own hand-written recipe book, recording half a century's combinations. This basic recipe is a starting point from which you can begin your own decades of experimentation...

INGREDIENTS
1.5 kg chosen fruit or vege
1 kg onions
½ cup ginger (Pat prefers crystallised, but you could
    use freshly grated ginger or 4 tsp ground ginger
    instead)
1 litre malt vinegar
2 cups sultanas
2 cups brown sugar
4–5 tsp spices (to suit your fruit or vege)
2 Tbsp salt

1) Peel, chop and de-seed fruit or vege as appropriate. Chop onions and ginger. (Pat simply pops everything in a food processor to speed things up.)

2) Combine all ingredients in a large saucepan and bring to the boil, stirring constantly.

3) Simmer for 1 to 1½ hours, or until thick.

4) Pour into prepared jars and seal. There's your next round of gifts sorted!

Pat says: 'Ideally, you should keep your chutney for a month before you use it — to allow the flavours to settle in.'

TIP: Pat's current favourite chutney is feijoa, spiced with ground cloves and curry power.

basic pickle

The ancient art of pickling dates back thousands of years, and was one of the best methods of keeping veges before refrigeration. These days we pickle mostly for flavour, but if you don't like to go without your favourite vege during the off-season, pickling remains a good way to keep it in supply.

You can get as creative as you like when pickling: pickle one type of vegetable, or make a mixed pickle by combining several varieties. Cucumbers, cabbages, cauliflowers, onions, peppers, carrots, choko, mushrooms, lemons, gherkins… With this basic generic recipe, the pickling world is your oyster!

INGREDIENTS
1 to 1.5 kg of your chosen veges or fruit

FOR BRINE
6-8 Tbsp salt
1 litre water

FOR SPICED VINEGAR
1 litre white vinegar
1 Tbsp cloves
1 Tbsp peppercorns
1 Tbsp mixed spice
2 tsp grated ginger
1 cinnamon stick
2 bay leaves

1) To make a strong brine, stir the salt into the water until it dissolves.

2) Chop up veges or fruit, and soak in the brine overnight.

3) Drain the veges or fruit, and rinse well with cold water.

4) Pack the veges or fruit into clean, prepared jars (see p. 69), making sure you leave about 2 cm free at the top.

TIP: Technically, brine is a pickle in itself – the salt acts as a preservative – so if you wish you can pour brine directly into the jars over your veges or fruit, and seal. Fresh green beans and carrots are good this way. If you're looking for more of a pickle-tasting pickle, continue with the next steps.

5) Make spiced vinegar by combining ingredients in a saucepan and bringing to the boil, stirring constantly. Simmer for several minutes.

6) Cover the veges or fruit with the spiced vinegar, still leaving 1 cm clear at the top for expansion.

7) Put the lid on your jar(s). Store for 2-4 weeks before eating, to allow the flavours to be absorbed.

Kept in the fridge, your pickles should last several months (if you haven't eaten them all by then).

preserved fruit

Imagine the satisfaction of dipping into a sweet jar of syrupy goodness on a winter's day, made from the bounty of summer…

It may sound like the opening of a dated TV show, about people who lead impossibly cottagey lives, but no — it could be you! Preserving fruit is a lot easier than you think.

INGREDIENTS
1 kg fruit
1.5 cups sugar (approx. — optional)
3 cups water (approx.)

Quantities will vary depending on how much fruit you have. You really need a kilogram or more of fruit to make preserving worthwhile.

Mary says: 'Get to know your greengrocer or local supermarket. They're often keen to get rid of very ripe fruit and may give it to you cheaply or even for free.'

1) Slice fruit in half, and remove stones (if applicable). You can also preserve the fruit whole if you prefer. If preserving whole, prick the skins with a needle to stop the fruit bursting and to allow the syrup to seep in.

2) Make a syrup by combining the sugar and water, at a ratio of about 1 cup sugar to 2 cups water. Heat slowly over a low heat, and stir until the sugar has dissolved.

Pat says: 'I like a sweet syrup, but you can reduce the sugar a little if you want to.'

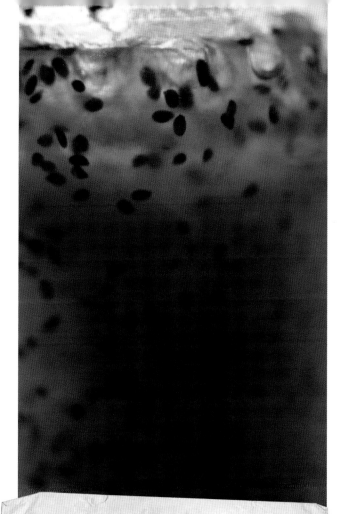

3) Add the fruit to the syrup. Continue to heat gently for several minutes.

4) Spoon into prepared jars until overflowing. Remove any air bubbles by sliding a knife or spatula around the inside of the jar between the edge of the glass and the fruit.

5) Wipe excess syrup from the rim and seal the lid. Keep the jars in the fridge.

TIP: Make sure the syrup covers the fruit completely.

Pat's jellies

Mary says: 'There's nobody makes a Jelly like Pat!'

Pat's fruit jellies are quick off the shelves at the Save the Children shop. I was surprised to find out how little effort it takes to make each jelly. Like 'Nana's Marmalade' and 'Easy Jam' (pp. 55 and 59), they rely on the traditional method of using natural pectin to set the fruit. Simple ingredients, no rocket science required.

INGREDIENTS
fruit (at least 1 kg)
water
sugar

Amounts will vary depending on how much fruit you have and how much jelly you want to make. Almost any fruit will make a good jelly, but quince and feijoa are two of Pat's favourites.

TIP: You can preserve fruit entirely sugar-free if you want to. Follow the same instructions, omitting the sugar altogether or replacing with honey (to taste). Use fruit that is not quite ripe as this will hold its flavour and colour better. You can use plain water, or replace it with fruit juice or wine for sweetness.

1) Chop, peel and de-seed your fruit.

2) Stew the fruit, by cooking it in a little water until soft.

3) Mash well.

4) Place a sieve over a bowl, and line the sieve with muslin or cotton cloth (e.g. a pillowcase, see p. 103). Pour in the mashed fruit.

5) Leave the fruit overnight to strain slowly into the bowl.

TIP: An unused disposable dishcloth will also do the trick if you don't have muslin.

Mary says: 'Pat has the patience of Job to make this — I always get bored and squeeze the cloth!'

Pat says: 'Don't do it during the day, Mary — that's the problem. Just put it in overnight, go to bed, wake up and it's done.'

6) Measure the juice in the bowl and add sugar, matching juice and sugar cup for cup.

7) Bring to the boil, stirring, and simmer for up to half an hour.

Pat says: 'Test it every ten minutes or it might set like glue!'

8) Test jelly as you would marmalade or jam (pp. 56 and 60), and pour into prepared jars when ready (see p. 69).

Preparing Jars

Many supermarkets and craft stores sell jars for homemade products, or — even better — you can recycle used jars. Whether recycled or not, follow these steps carefully.

1) Wash the jars well in fresh hot water before you begin.

2) When you start to cook the preserve, place the open jars in the oven at the minimum heat setting. Remove when ready to pour in the preserve. This both warms the jars ready for the product, and helps to sterilise them.

no lids? no problem

Pre-packaged cellophane rounds for jars without lids can be found at most supermarkets. Otherwise simply cut a piece of cellophane into rounds, big enough to comfortably cover the openings of the jars you are using. Moisten the cellophane rounds, press tightly over the jar openings and hold in place with a rubber band.

TIP: If you want your jams and jellies to keep for longer, pour a layer of molten wax over the top before you seal the jar. The molten wax sets solid, can be easily removed and will stop your preserves going mouldy. You can buy special preserving wax, but Pat and Mary say candle wax does the job just fine. Be careful when melting down the wax though — Pat left it alone once and nearly set the house on fire!

CHAPTER FOUR

Time for a Tipple

Brewing with Mary

Mary's honey mead

INGREDIENTS

4 litres water
500 ml honey
125 g sugar
juice and sliced peel of 1 orange (optional)
60 g yeast
warm water

1) Combine the water, honey and sugar in a pot and bring to the boil, stirring constantly.

2) Skim the frothy bits off the top and pour the rest into a large ceramic casserole dish or Crockpot to cool.

3) When lukewarm, stir in the orange juice and sliced orange peel.

4) Mix the yeast with a little warm water and add this to the mixture.

5) Cover the dish with a lid, and leave it to 'work' for about 2-3 weeks. Stir twice a day for the first few days.

TIP: Keep the dish at room temperature, and try not to move it around.

6) When the yeast settles to the bottom and the mead looks quite clear, it's ready to bottle. Strain through a fine sieve or cloth, and bottle.

When Mary Allan first got married, she had to contend with a 'terrible old laundry'. But somewhere along the line, her husband John took a fancy to making home brew beer in the old washing machine tub — which made things seem a little better! Mary was pleased when John turned his skills to brewing honey mead instead, because 'at least that's good for you'. It was potent too: just half a glass and John would be asleep, Mary remembers nostalgically.

This traditional honey mead recipe is hop-free, meaning it's very easy to make — and you quite possibly already have the ingredients in your cupboard.

7) Keep your mead in bottles for a good 3 months before drinking.

BOTTLING

If you, like me, have always been a little intimidated by the complex bottling procedures required for home brew, fear not! Traditional mead-making is far less involved.

Provided you have left the mead long enough to ensure the yeast has finished working, you should be able to avoid the case of the exploding bottle.

1) Pour the strained mead into empty, sterilised wine bottles or swing-top glass bottles. The easiest way to prepare bottles is to run them through a dishwasher cycle.

2) If you have swing-top bottles, swing in the top and secure it. Easy.

3) If you have wine bottles, stop them with a cork pushed as far in as you can get it. You could be fancy and use a hand-corker if you have access to one, but if not, do like our grandparents did and just bash it in with a rubber or wooden mallet. Do this carefully

— don't smash the bottle! It's a good idea to tie corks down with wire or twine to avoid a surprise cork rocket.

4) You can use screw tops on modern wine bottles, but make extra certain your yeast has finished working, and that the lid — as well as the bottle — has been thoroughly cleaned.

5) If the idea of exploding glass is just too scary, use plastic soft drink bottles as you would for ginger beer (see p. 78).

TIP: It's a good idea to use a funnel unless your dish has a pourer, or you'll end up wearing a lot of the mead. MAKE SURE YOU LEAVE ONE CENTIMETRE OF HEAD-ROOM AT THE TOP OF THE BOTTLE!

TIP: Despite all precautions, creating a small accidental grenade is still not out of the question - especially if you are new to brewing. Bear this in mind when storing bottles (especially glass). I recommend the shed, or other areas of limited human habitation.

Sipping Elderflowers with Jenni's Nan

It is said that summer hasn't truly started until the elderflower is in bloom, and it ends when the elderberries are ripe. Elder bushes grow prolifically in many countries, and their scented flowers and berries can be used in countless different recipes. In recent decades the poor elder has gone largely ignored and unrecognised, but it's starting to regain the kind of popularity it enjoyed in Nana's day.

Elder bushes grow rapidly and are sometimes removed from gardens because of this, but kept in check they are brilliant to have around. They are distinguished by large clusters of little white flowers, which make way for berries in late summer. They often grow wild, and can be found on roadsides and in parks. Best not to pick from roadside plants though, as they may have been sprayed or covered in traffic fumes.

Jenni Long's Nan lives with Jenni's parents in a picturesque cottage (you know, the kind with flourishing herbs and woodland creatures prancing across the garden). Jenni's Nan has long been a connoisseur of the elderflower, and recently the family has been popping the corks on the elderflower champagne they bottled last month. Elderflower champagne is easy to make, beautifully refreshing and ready to drink just two weeks after bottling. Not surprisingly, it's Nan's favourite elder recipe!

TIP: When picking your flowers, try to find clusters that are facing the sun and fully opened. Avoid browning blossom as this can affect the taste.

elderflower champagne

INGREDIENTS
4 or more large clusters (heads) of elderflowers
2 lemons
1 kg sugar (or honey)
4 Tbsp white wine vinegar
10 litres cold water
½ tsp dried yeast (optional)

1) Wash the flowers, removing any cobwebs or bugs trying to hide amongst them.

2) Wash and squeeze the lemons, and peel off the rind as thinly as possible using a potato peeler.

3) Put the flowers, lemon juice and rind into a large plastic bucket or container. Make sure it has been thoroughly washed in hot water.

4) Slowly add the sugar and vinegar, being careful not to crush the flowers with the sugar.

5) Pour in the water and stir gently. Cover the bucket and leave to stand for 24 hours, stirring every 6 hours or so. If you don't notice signs of fermenting (bubbles or froth on top), add ½ tsp of dried yeast and leave to stand another day.

6) Strain and bottle the mixture as you would for Mary's honey mead (see p. 72). Store the bottles in a cool place.

7) Elderflower champagne is ready after just 2 weeks! The flavour does improve with age though, and can be used much later. The drink should be fizzy and is mildly alcoholic.

elderflower cordial

If you're after a non-alcoholic, less effervescent option, elderflower cordial is the way to go. It's also excellent in cocktails.

INGREDIENTS

20 elderflower heads

4 cups sugar (ideally caster sugar)

1.5 litres water (boiling)

2 lemons (juiced and sliced)

1 orange (sliced or chopped)

50 g citric acid (available from the pharmacy or health store)

1) Wash the flowers to remove any dirt and those hiding bugs.

2) Place the sugar in a heatproof bowl and pour the boiling water on top. Give it a good stir, and leave to cool down.

3) Add the fruit, citric acid and flowers.

4) Leave for 24 hours in a cool spot.

Jenni says: 'Pop in and give it a stir now and then to let it know you care.'

5) Strain and bottle as you would for elderflower champagne (no need to worry about glass explosions with this one though!)

6) Keep your cordial in the fridge. Dilute with water or serve over ice.

TIP: Once autumn is on its way, and you've enjoyed all your Elderflower Champagne, try using ripe elderberries to make John's 'Easy Jam' or 'Pat's Jellies' (pp. 59 and 65).

Lushings of Ginger Beer

homemade ginger beer

INGREDIENTS

1 cup sugar
2 Tbsp warm water
¼ tsp dried yeast
juice and grated rind of 2 lemons
1 tsp-1 Tbsp dried ginger (to taste)
a good chunk of fresh ginger (grated — optional)
1 cup boiling water
water (cool)

1) Dissolve half a teaspoon of the sugar in the warm water, add the yeast, and stir. Set aside — preferably somewhere warm.

2) Place the lemon juice and grated rind in a large jug with the remaining sugar and dried and fresh ginger, and pour the boiling water on top, to cover.

3) Leave it to think about itself for 10 minutes.

4) Strain the mixture into an empty 1.5 litre plastic bottle — this will become your bottle of ginger beer.

Stef says: 'Washed recycled soft drink bottles with a screw top are perfect for this job. Please don't go using glass ones like my nana did!'

Stefanie Lash's Nana, Nancy, was an inveterate bottler of pretty much anything. There was never a dull moment for the young Stef after Nana moved in — and always an abundance of homemade ginger beer. Nana Nancy would mix up a brew and leave it in the hot water cupboard until it fermented to within an inch of its life — and the family's lives too, if she was using glass bottles! Stef still reminisces nostalgically about the sound of ginger beer bottles exploding in the middle of the night. Ginger beer is easy and fun to make, and better for you than the kind you'll find at the store. If there are kids in the house they'll love watching the mixture change as it brews, and the anticipation of tasting their first glass of the real thing. Luckily, these days you can use plastic bottles...

There are several ways of making ginger beer. This Lash family favourite is very simple, and has been well and truly tested over the generations.

TIP: Even with plastic bottles, over-eager ginger beer may explode if left too long. Check it regularly, and think about where you store it. Next to your best linen, paperwork or favourite artwork is probably not wise!

5) Top up the bottle with cool water until almost full, making sure to leave a little room at the top. The bottle should feel lukewarm.

6) Add the yeast mixture to the bottle as soon as it shows signs of action — bubbling or foaming.

7) Screw the cap on the bottle tightly, give it a good swirl to mix and set aside in a warm place.

8) This ginger beer can take anywhere from 1-5 days to brew, depending on the virility of your yeast. Squeeze the bottle now and then to test it. If it's rock hard and can't be dented, it should be good and ready.

9) Chill thoroughly, and open very slowly!

ginger beer cocktails

Nana Nancy was apparently a bit of a party girl in her day, always up for a do. She replaced the TV in her living room with a billiard table, and guests were always welcome. Raising four kids on a dairy farm meant making your own fun, and Nancy was a dab hand at whipping up a cocktail. Ginger beer was one of her favourite ingredients (if the bottles were still intact). It marries well with most fruit flavours — especially apple and berries — and with a wide range of spirits, such as vodka, bourbon, cachaça, rum... It's a great mixer for all seasons, so whether you're sipping a winter punch by the fire or smuggling a ginger mule into a summer festival, you can't go wrong!

Nancy May

Nana Nancy's favourite.

40 ml scotch or bourbon
40 ml ginger beer (see p. 78)

Serve in a short glass over ice, or top up with more ginger beer and serve in a tall glass for a milder hit.

Classic Moscow Mule

15 ml lime juice
handful fresh mint leaves
2 tsp sugar
60 ml vodka
ice
ginger beer (see p. 78)
lime wedge, to serve

Muddle the lime juice and mint leaves with the sugar and vodka, and strain into a tall glass of ice. Top up with ginger beer and serve with a lime wedge. Tastes like summer!

Stef says: 'Add a little fresh raspberry, cranberry or strawberry Juice if you're in the mood for something pink.'

Tropical Mule

For a mid summer mocktail treat, this is hard to beat.

1.5 litres ginger beer (see p. 78)
750 ml pineapple juice
ice
fresh pineapple pieces
fresh kiwifruit pieces
few handfuls fresh mint

In a large jug, mix a bottle of your ginger beer with half as much pineapple juice and loads of ice. Add chopped pineapple and kiwifruit pieces, and a few handfuls of fresh mint. Picnic, anyone…?

Stef says: 'If you fancy something stronger, replace half the pineapple Juice with vodka and that should take you through to the wee, small hours.'

Dark and Stormy

The clouds may be gathering, but if there's ginger beer in your cupboard there's still a cocktail to be had.

120 ml dark rum
ginger beer (see p. 78)
lime and sugar to taste
lots of ice

Combine all ingredients in a tall glass.

Stef says: 'The flavours in a Dark and Stormy are clean and few, so use good-quality rum if you have it.'

TIP: These cocktails work well with either homemade or store-bought ginger beer. If you're using a bought one go easy on the sugar, as commercial brands are usually much sweeter.

Winter Punch

This spicy punch can be served either warm or cold, and is perfect for a mid winter fireside get together. A bit of Winter Punch, and spring will arrive in no time!

½ cup sugar
100 ml water
2.5 litres ginger beer (see p. 78)
750 ml bottle of whisky or bourbon
750 ml apple juice
small chunk (about 2½ cm) of fresh ginger, pulped
fresh lime juice (to taste)
lime wedges
½ tsp nutmeg
½ tsp star anise

Gently heat the sugar with the water until dissolved. Mix along with the rest of the ingredients in a large punch bowl, garnishing with the lime and spices. Leave to stand at room temperature for a while to let the flavours emerge. Chill, or heat gently to serve.

Grandma Marygold Millar has always been a maker and a doer. She is infamous amongst her family for having once made 365 jars of preserved fruit, to ensure her husband and children had fruit every night of the year! In recent years however she has become better known for her wonderful home-grown teas.

Her granddaughter, Vic, remembers Grandma coming to live with the family. Vic would climb up into her bed and they'd watch TV together, drinking hot chocolate and eating biscuits. On hot summer days Vic would shelter in the shed, and gaze at all the drying tea leaves that Marygold had strung up on a line. Her specialty was mint tea, which the young Vic hated and wouldn't touch. But, now that she's been a grown-up for a few years, Vic has developed quite a taste for it — and Marygold delights in regularly sending her little tins of dried peppermint leaves.

Even if your only garden space is a windowsill, you can grow your own fresh herbal teas. Many of the plants that make good tea grow easily, and are pot friendly.

mint tea

Mint tea — peppermint in particular — is Marygold's favourite. Peppermint has all kinds of medicinal values, and has long been used as a natural soother for stomach upsets and indigestion. A hot cup of mint tea is refreshing and calming. You won't have any trouble growing mint, indoors or out. In fact it's better to keep it in pots either way because it grows like a weed in the garden, and can take over if you turn your back for a week or two. Make sure to keep it watered — particularly in the heat of summer — but don't let it get too soggy. Choose from many different kinds of mint, such as spearmint, peppermint, orange mint and chocolate mint. Several varieties (including peppermint) are hybrids, so it's rare to find true seeds. Buy seedlings, or take cuttings from friends' plants (see p. 32).

To make mint tea: Simply pour boiling water over the crushed, dried leaves, and allow to steep for a maximum of 10 minutes. Strain and serve, sweetening with honey if you wish. Use about 1 tsp leaves per cup of water. You can also use fresh leaves (about 1 Tbsp), but tear and crush them a little first to release the good stuff.

parsley tea

Parsley, the wonder herb (see p. 50), makes a surprisingly good tea. Yet another reason to grow it! As a tea it's good for freshening the breath and packs an excellent vitamin punch. It's also good for the urinary tract (just what you always wanted). Women should steer clear of it when pregnant or breastfeeding though as larger quantities can stimulate uterine contractions and reduce milk supply.

To make parsley tea: Use fresh leaves if you can. Unlike many teas, parsley tea works best with fresh foliage. Take 2 Tbsp chopped fresh leaves and/or stems, and follow the instructions for mint tea. If using dried parsley, reduce the quantity to 2 tsp.

chamomile tea

Chamomile is a type of marigold that makes a great companion plant to others if you have a garden (see p. 31). It doesn't mind growing in pots, but does like to sunbathe and feel the wind in its hair — so if you live in an apartment it'll do better on the balcony than the windowsill. Give it lots to drink in summer as you would for mint. If you plant chamomile in the garden it will happily seed itself, so you should get a continuous crop from year to year. Chamomile tea is famous for calming the nerves and helping you sleep — a good bedtime cuppa.

To make chamomile tea: Use the flowers of the chamomile plant, not the leaves. Brew as per mint tea (see p. 83), preferably with dried rather than fresh flowers.

lemon balm tea

Lemon balm is related to mint and has similarly hardy growing habits. Start your lemon balm from a cutting, or plant a seedling, and it will almost take care of itself. It's excellent as a cooking herb (marries well with seafood), and makes a great tea both on its own or mixed with other ingredients. It's said to boost immunity and relieve headaches, and you can even apply it externally on itchy bites or summer rashes! Keep a brew in the fridge for when you run out of Calendula Cream (p. 114). Its lemony taste makes it accessible for kids and novice herbal tea drinkers.

To make lemon balm tea: Brew as per mint tea (see p. 83).

TIP: Take care not to pick too much of your plant! If your appetite for tea exceeds the limits of your crop, plant another so that both plants can withstand your harvesting.

drying your leaves

There are several ways of doing this. Choose the method that best suits you and your home space. Once dried, herbs can be stored for up to a year in jars or tins.

• On a line: Tie bunches of dried herbs together and hang them upside down on a line (a piece of taut string will do). Find a spot that is dark, warm and dry with good airflow.
• In the oven: Spread leaves, flowers or stems onto a sheet of baking paper and place in the oven at the minimum temperature. Leave the oven door slightly open. It will take your herbs a few hours to dry, so this is not a great option for power conservation! Remove herbs when they are completely dry and leave to cool down before storing.
• In the microwave: Spread leaves, flowers or stems onto a paper towel and microwave on low for a minute. Keep doing this, checking every minute, until the herbs are nearly but not quite dry. Leave out overnight to finish off. This method is quick and easy, but may reduce the nutrient content of your tea.
• In a dehydrator (if available): A fruit dehydrator will dry the leaves nicely.
• With patience: Separate leaves, flowers or stems and spread onto a sheet of baking paper. Store somewhere dark, warm and dry until ready. How long this takes will depend a lot on your local climate.

Marygold says: 'Test your herbs for dryness by rubbing them between your thumb and finger. If they feel brittle and crumbly, they are ready.'

CHAPTER FIVE

Rocking the Kitchen

Making Stock with Marion

arion McLeod laughs that her Scottish heritage led to her inability to waste anything. In good McLeod tradition, even the water she used to boil the veges is drained into a jug and stowed in the fridge, waiting for its opportunity to be re-used. A golden opportunity for using it occurs when making stock.

Marion grew up in the south of New Zealand (the original landing place of many a hardy Scot), and she remembers that the bones and leftover scraps from the traditional Sunday roast were turned into stock and rissoles the next day. Nowadays most of us wouldn't think twice before throwing our leftovers to the dog, and later using a spoonful of impossibly coloured stock powder to flavour our cooking. But no more! Not once you discover how easy and delicious it is to make your own fresh liquid stock (including vegetarian).

Marion's stock

The beauty of stock is that it can be made with pretty much any leftovers, whether they're wilting vegetables in the fridge tray, bones from the roast you lovingly made for the family the night before, or the remains of a cooked chook you grabbed from the supermarket to scoff between meetings. No one cares how you got it — just don't waste it!

INGREDIENTS FOR CHICKEN, BEEF, LAMB OR PORK STOCK

leftover bits and bones of chicken, beef, lamb or pork
leftover gravy (if there is any)
1 onion (or even a half will do)
1-2 carrots
celery, or celery ends and leaves

bay leaf, if available
other fresh herbs if desired (e.g. parsley, thyme)
1–2 Tbsp whole peppercorns
salt (to taste)

INGREDIENTS FOR FISH STOCK
fish bones, heads and tails (white-fleshed fish is best for
   stock. Oily fish is a bit, well, oily)
1–2 onions
assorted herbs (whatever you like, e.g. parsley, bay leaf,
   thyme)
1–2 Tbsp whole peppercorns

INGREDIENTS FOR VEGETABLE STOCK
leftover veges, including ends and stalks
1–2 onions (or 3 if you're keen!)
bay leaves (if you have them)
assorted herbs (whatever you like, e.g. parsley, thyme,
   oregano)
1–2 Tbsp whole peppercorns
salt (to taste)

Marion says: 'A leftover potato or a dear departed kumara is good to add too, as it will thicken the stock.'

1) Put your chosen ingredients (except salt) into a large pot. The veges can be chopped as roughly as you like, no one's going to see them! Don't be afraid to use leftover ends, stalks and leaves — it all adds to the flavour, as does meat fat.

2) Fill the pot with water, just covering your ingredients.

3) Cover and bring to the boil.

4) Reduce heat and simmer for at least 1–1½ hours.

TIP: If you have a slow cooker or Crockpot, you could just chuck everything in there and leave it on high for six to eight hours.

5) Strain the stock through a sieve into a large bowl. Use a fine sieve, or even some muslin or cotton if making fish stock, to catch the tiny bones.

6) *Now* you can throw out the bits and bones!

7) Add salt to taste.

8) Leave stock to cool, ideally overnight. Any fat will rise to the surface and can easily be scraped off.

9) You're done! How easy was that? Enjoy using your stock to make fantastic-tasting soups, stews and other meals.

Marion says: 'I love the homely smell of stock when it's cooking. It makes everything so cosy — especially in winter.'

TIP: Add a little lemon zest to give your stock some zing.

TIP: Celery is excellent for flavouring stocks and soups, and also makes a good snack. To stop it wilting in the fridge, wrap it in tinfoil.

TIP: If you have frugal tendencies, use the water you saved (of course) when you drained yesterday's veges. It will add even more vege goodness to your stock.

TIP: Freeze in portions to use anytime.

Pasta with Drew

Andrew Munro is not the first person you'd think to turn to for domestic handy hints. He lives in an inner-city bachelor pad with three other guys, can usually be found with a beer in one hand, and is the type of 'young lad' your Nana probably disapproves of. But after an (abandoned) attempt to study acting, and a stint as MC in a strip club, Drew decided it was time to get serious about his career. He took a course, became a good chef, and went on to work for several years in an Italian restaurant. Needless to say, pasta is his specialty!

These days Drew is picking up starring roles in television commercials, but luckily for us, he shared his pasta knowledge first. No pasta ever tastes quite as good as fresh pasta — and, once you discover how easy it is to make, you won't need to buy the expensive version.

Drew's fresh pasta

INGREDIENTS
200 g flour
2 eggs
20 ml olive oil
1 tsp salt

1) Pour the flour into a bowl, and make a well in the middle.

2) Put the remaining ingredients into the well.

3) Mix to form a dough.

Drew says: 'The dough should be fairly "rubbery", and shouldn't stick to the sides of the bowl. If it feels tacky to touch, add a little more flour.'

4) Roll the dough by hand into a ball. Cover with cling-film, and place in the fridge for about 20 minutes.

Drew says: 'This is so the fibres of the dough can relax — chill out a bit.'

TIP: The best way to roll is to start in the middle of the dough, roll one way, turn the board around and roll the other. This will keep the dough stronger than if you roll all the way up and down each time. Make sure your rolling pin is dry.

5) On a lightly floured board, roll out the dough with a rolling pin until it is pretty thin — about the thickness of the cardboard on a cereal packet.

Drew says: 'If you don't have a rolling pin, use a wine bottle. Weigh it down with some water inside if it has a screw top — or use a full one!'

6) Cut your pasta into whatever shapes you wish, boil uncovered for about 5 minutes, and serve with your favourite pasta sauce (see p. 48 for a simple sauce).

This recipe makes enough for 2 adults. You can easily adapt it at a ratio of 100 g of flour per person.

cutting shapes

Though a pasta machine makes things easier, you don't necessarily need one to make good pasta. Here are some basic ways to cut your favourite type by hand.

For fettucine or tagliatelle: Cut the rolled dough into long, thin strips.

For farfalle: Cut the rolled dough into small squares (about three or four centimetres) and pinch them in the middle to form a bow shape.

For lasagne: Cut the rolled dough into large rectangular sheets (sized to suit).

For ravioli: Cut the rolled dough into two large squares of equal size. Place your chosen filling in evenly spaced blobs on one square, and brush the dough with a little cold water. Lie the other square on top, and press the layers together between mounds. Cut along the pressed bits to get squares of ravioli.

TIP: Fresh pasta freezes well. Try making a bigger batch and freezing in portions for easy meals.

Baking for Non-bakers

Even if you're not a kitchen type, there are some recipes from our grandparents' generation that anyone can make and everyone should know. Gone are the days of arriving at a potluck with a packet of corn chips you grabbed from the store on the way. Gone too are the days when pulling a block of chocolate from the cupboard counted as a homemade dessert. Now you can make your Nana proud, and your guests (or date or kids or mates) very happy!

Mavis is a retirement home resident these days, but can still whip up a dessert at the drop of a hat. With eighteen grandchildren, she's had plenty of practice! Mavis reckons recipes have got a bit fancy-pants these days: why make something complicated, when something simple tastes just as delicious?

Mavis's Fruit Crumble

This gluten-free recipe can be made with pretty much any fruit you have in stock, including the kind that comes in cans. Get creative with your combinations.

INGREDIENTS
3 cups fruit (or about 2 regular 400 g cans)
sprinkling of brown sugar (optional)
2½ cups rolled oats
150 g butter (melted)
1 Tbsp brown sugar

1) Preheat oven to 180°C.

2) If you are using fresh fruit, peel it and chop it into bite-sized pieces. Put it in a saucepan with a little water or juice to cover, and a sprinkling of brown sugar if desired, and stew until tender. This takes anywhere between 10–20 minutes, depending on how firm your fruit is (e.g. apples will take longer than berries).

Mavis says: 'Keep checking and stirring to prevent an evening spent scrubbing all hell out of your saucepan.'

3) Put the stewed or canned fruit into an oven-proof casserole dish and set aside.

4) In a bowl, mix the oats with the butter and brown sugar until it roughly resembles breadcrumbs. If it feels too dry, add more butter; if it seems a little sticky or moist, add more oats.

TIP: Don't worry too much about the crumble mixture. This is a pretty forgiving recipe – unless it's dripping wet, it'll probably turn out fine.

5) Sprinkle the crumble mixture over the fruit, and place the dish in the oven. Bake uncovered for about 20 minutes, or until the crumble starts to turn golden.

TIP: If you're using frozen fruit, don't defrost first – the moisture will be useful during cooking. Similarly there's no need to drain tinned fruit – tip the whole lot in.

Lawrence's Fruitcake

Bernice Gleadow (see p. 51) says of her late hus-band, Lawrence, 'You hear people say they have hyperactive children, well I had a hyperactive hus-band!' Bernice cooked the family meals throughout much of their marriage, but in his last two years Lawrence took over the kitchen. He even talked of writing a recipe book one day. This fruitcake reci-pe was one of Lawrence's favourites, and deserves its moment of glory. It is the simplest you'll ever find (with only three ingredients!) — yet it tastes elaborate. This fruitcake is great for any occasion, but particularly good for impressing the family at Christmas.

INGREDIENTS
1 kg mixed dried fruit and peel (fruit mix)
2 cups leftover beverage (e.g. tea, juice, wine, cordial)
2–3 cups self-raising flour

1) Place the fruit mix in a bowl. Cover with the liquid, and leave overnight to soak.

TIP: The liquid can be anything you have lying around: the remains of a bottle of juice, soft drink or wine, cold tea from the teapot, or even a combination!

2) The next day, preheat the oven to 200°C.

3) Line a large cake tin with baking paper.

4) Gently mix the flour into the fruit mixture until combined.

Lawrence says: 'Two cups of flour will make a lovely rich cake, while 3 cups makes a very pleasant afternoon tea cake.'

TIP: If you don't have self-raising flour, just use plain flour and add 1 tsp baking powder per cup of flour.

5) Pour into the lined cake tin.

TIP: For an extra-special finish, sprinkle sunflower seeds, chopped walnuts or cherries on top of the cake before baking.

6) Turn the oven down to 150°C, and bake the cake for about 1½ hrs. Test with a skewer: if it comes out sticky, turn the oven off, but leave the cake in for another ½ hour or so.

7) Turn onto a cake rack to cool.

TIP: If you wish, drizzle some diluted brandy over the cake before serving.

Lawrence says: 'Do not dilute the brandy for the cook!'

Cultural Explorations

If only I had met Debbie ter Borg years ago, I wouldn't have spent so much money on commercial yoghurts. Debbie has been teaching people how to culture their own for years. Her passion for homemade and home-grown foods originated in the 1970s, when she came upon a book about whole foods while working as a librarian. Debbie can still visualise the moment when she saw the book on the shelf. So began a journey of learning as much as she possibly could, and rediscovering skills that she remembered her great-grandmother having in abundance.

Debbie's tried-and-true yoghurt recipe is ridiculously simple, and tastes like the thick, expensive Greek-style yoghurt available in the shops. No need for special equipment — anyone can do this!

Debbie's homemade yoghurt

You can start your yoghurt from any commercial yoghurt that contains only milk and cultures (e.g. L. acidophilus, L. Bulgaricus, etc.) — check the ingredients list on the label. Even better, you can use a spoonful of carefully cultured yoghurt that a friend or yoghurt-loving neighbour has kept going. Debbie has kept hers going for over twenty-five years! If using a good strong culture, reduce the amount to a quarter of a teaspoon.

INGREDIENTS
1 litre milk (to make 1 litre yoghurt)
2 tsp yoghurt (containing only milk and cultures)

1) 'Scald' the milk. No, this does not mean burn it! It means pour the milk into a saucepan, and stir until it begins to bubble up.

2) Remove from heat, and set aside to cool.

3) Put the existing yoghurt (commercial or home-cultured) into a clean jar.

TIP: Make sure your jar is big enough! If making one litre of yoghurt, then — um — you'll need a one litre jar...

4) When the milk has cooled to about 40-43°C, pour it into the jar on top of the yoghurt.

Debbie says: 'You can use a thermometer for this, but you don't have to. When you can touch the base of the saucepan and it feels hot, but doesn't burn, the milk is ready.'

TIP: If a skin has formed on the milk, don't hyperventilate — this is meant to happen! Just give it a stir.

5) Seal the jar and place it in a chilly bin (aka cooler, cool box, Esky) beside another jar full of hot water. Debbie uses a small chilly bin, just big enough to hold the two jars — if yours is bigger, stuff the spare space with newspaper. It's also a good idea to wrap the jars in a tea towel.

TIP: Don't have a chilly bin? No worries. Stuff a cardboard box with scrunched up newspaper, leaving just enough room for your two jars. Once your jars are in, cover with more newspaper to insulate. You can also try using the hot water cupboard, if you have one, or a commercial yoghurt-making Thermos.

6) Leave for 24 hours.

7) Eat your lovely yoghurt! To sweeten, add a spoonful of honey or maple syrup, or your favourite jam, to add a fruity twist.

TIP: If your yoghurt doesn't seem quite set and is 'gloopy', you probably poured the milk in when it was too cool. If it has separated into uneven layers, the milk was probably too hot. Use this batch as a culture to start a new one, and put it down to experience. There may be a bit of trial and error involved with the first couple of batches.

TIP: You may notice that a creamy layer has formed on the top of your yoghurt. This is sour cream! Scoop it off and use in place of butter, or however you like to eat it.

Labna Cheese

Once you have made your own yoghurt, it's very easy to make soft Labna Cheese. Even if you can't summon the energy to make your own yoghurt, you can still make this cheese from bought yoghurt (make sure it's Greek-style).

INGREDIENTS
homemade yoghurt (or Greek-style yoghurt)
fresh herbs, salt and pepper, to taste

1) Place a sieve over a saucepan, and line it with muslin or fine cloth. Debbie simply cuts up an old (clean) cotton pillowcase — great way to recycle!

2) Pour the yoghurt into the cloth, and tie the ends together to form a bag.

3) Hang up the cloth bag and leave overnight.

4) Serve your cheese with crackers and fruit to impress your guests!

Debbie says: 'Before you serve, mix in some fresh herbs, salt or pepper if desired. Get creative — the sky's the limit!'

TIP: If you have nowhere to hang your bag, tie the knot around a wooden spoon and balance across a basket or cardboard box. That way it's also portable, which could be handy in a small house or apartment.

CHAPTER SIX

Life's Rich Tapestry

Marcella's Home Cleaning

Marcella Cotton's grown-up children have regular debates as to which of them is going to inherit her household maintenance notebook. It may not sound like the sort of item to cause a family feud, but it is indeed an indispensable treasure. Over the years, Marcella has compiled countless tips on how to keep house — as her mother and grandmother did before her. What makes her notes so prized is that her methods are easy and efficient, and include recipes for homemade cleaning products that you can whip up in under a minute from ingredients in the kitchen cupboard. Let's face it, cleaning is not usually a favourite pastime no matter what music you put on to distract yourself. But knowing you've created your own polish or spray that's entirely non-toxic (even edible!) and eco-friendly — and that it's saving you a truckload of cash in the supermarket's cleaning aisle — makes it somehow less onerous. Even (almost) fun.

Try these top six ideas next time you're faced with a spring clean. You can do almost all household cleaning with baking soda, lemon juice, vinegar and hot water.

easy-off oven cleaner

INGREDIENTS
baking soda (several Tbsp)
water (enough to make thick paste)

Judge the quantities according to the size of your oven.

1) Place the baking soda in a bowl, and add a little water until it resembles a thick paste.

2) 'Paint' this onto your oven with a pastry brush or — if you don't have a brush — smear on with a paper towel. Paint it generously everywhere apart from the elements.

3) Heat the oven to a moderate to high temperature for at least half an hour, leave to cool, then give it a good scrub and wipe off! No need to rinse.

Marcella says: 'The paste will look disgusting, but don't worry, it works.'

TIP: Paint the paste on just before you cook or bake something, and simply wipe off when you're done. The paste is non-toxic, doesn't smell, and won't affect your food.

TIP: This paste is also great for removing tough dirt or grease on kitchen and bathroom surfaces.

sparkling windows

INGREDIENTS
squirt of dishwashing liquid
hot water
old newspapers

1) Combine a dash of dishwashing liquid with hot water.

2) Crumple a piece of newspaper, dip it into the mixture and give your windows a good rub.

3) Crumple another piece of newspaper to dry and polish.

Newspaper will not only give you streak-free windows, but it also leaves a residue that acts as a dust repellent. Plus you're recycling! Why buy glass cleaner?

mould buster

INGREDIENT
white vinegar

White vinegar is a natural enemy of the pink mould that often develops in bathrooms and kitchens.

1) To blitz this mould, simply paint or spray white vinegar over the affected surfaces and leave overnight.

2) Rinse off in the morning.

3) The smell will quickly dissipate once the area is rinsed.

Marcella says: 'It doesn't smell great but, then again, neither does bleach — and vinegar does less harm.'

TIP: If you're germ-phobic don't panic. Marcella is an infection control nurse at a public hospital and knows what she is talking about. She recommends adding a little diluted antiseptic to your formula for surface and door handle cleaning during flu outbreaks and the like...

wonder wash

INGREDIENT
white vinegar

White vinegar is also the unsung hero of the laundry.

• Add ½ cup white vinegar to your rinse cycle in place of fabric softener to soften, brighten and reduce the lint on clothes. Excellent for sensitive skin.
• Soak whites and smelly or stained clothes in a bucket of warm water with 1 cup white vinegar before washing. Especially great for sweat stains, smelly socks, grease, and whites that are greying or yellow.
• Clean your washing machine now and then to remove grease and soap build-up by running it through an empty wash cycle with 1 cup white vinegar.

No, your clothes won't come out smelling like vinegar! Even if traces of the vinegar smell do remain, they will quickly disappear as the clothes dry.

furniture polish

INGREDIENTS
½ cup olive oil
juice of 2 lemons

1) Combine the olive oil with the lemon juice and give it a good shake to mix.

2) Rub onto wooden furniture with a cloth, then polish with a dry cloth.

The olive oil will protect the wood while the lemon juice handles any dirt and grease. The result is a shiny and smooth finish.

clear drains

INGREDIENTS
2 Tbsp baking soda
lemon juice or vinegar (optional)
hot water

Avoid pouring bleach down your drains. It can damage pipes, leave toxic residue and is on the environmental no-no list. Keep your drains free flowing and sweet smelling by using baking soda once a fortnight.

1) Spoon the baking soda into the drain.

2) Chase it with a dash of lemon juice or vinegar, or just enough hot water to wash it down.

3) Leave overnight, and flush with hot water in the morning.

Homemade Cosmetics

There's nothing wrong with having a little luxury in your life. Male or female, we all get a boost when our body feels great and we take the time to indulge in a touch of spa treatment! Shops know this, that's why their shelves are well stocked with every kind of expensive cosmetic and skin-enhancing concoction. If you worry about what's in them, can't afford them, want a more environmentally friendly alternative, or just fancy a quick project, do what Nana did and make your own! Here are some of my favourite homemade recipes, gathered from family and friends, which won't have you hunting for obscure ingredients.

Serena's Citrus Scrub

This decadent body scrub is a great way to use up discarded lemon or orange peel, which can't be used for composting. Mandarin and lime peel also work well.

INGREDIENTS
citrus fruit peelings
2 Tbsp rolled oats or wheat bran
milk
½ Tbsp honey (approx.)

1) Leave the citrus peelings somewhere away from sunlight — such as your hot water cupboard.

2) Dry completely, until they feel brittle (this can take a week or two)

3) Grind the dried peel into a powder, using a blender or mortar and pestle, if you have one.

TIP: Unless you really feel like a workout I recommend the blender...

4) Mix 2 Tbsp of this powder with rolled oats or wheat bran.

5) Add a little milk to moisten, and then the honey, stirring until combined.

6) Rub the coarse paste all over your body before a shower or bath. You'll come out feeling like Cleopatra!

TIP: For a quick, cheap exfoliant, simply squeeze some of your regular shower gel into the palm of your hand and add a spoonful of sugar — rub on, and wash off! Coarse salt in a few tablespoons of oil (e.g. olive oil, avocado oil) is also an excellent homemade moisturising exfoliant.

Nat's Body Butter

INGREDIENTS

1 cup oil (sweet almond or avocado are best, but even
   olive oil will work)
½ cup grated beeswax (found in organic shops and
   craft stores)
few drops essential oil (any scent, your choice)

1) Prepare a glass jar or container by washing it
thoroughly with hot water and placing it into an oven
at low temperature.

2) Combine the oil and beeswax in a saucepan, and stir
over a low heat until the beeswax has all melted.

3) Remove from heat and beat gently with a fork or
whisk until cool.

4) Stir in a few drops of your chosen essential oil, and
pour into the prepared jar.

> TIP: You can also stir in a teaspoon of
> Vitamin E oil for extra moisturising.

5) Store in a cool place. If you have very dry skin you
can even use this as a refreshing facial moisturiser, and
it makes an excellent 'man cream'.

> TIP: If you're using avocado oil you'll
> get a lovely dark green body butter – don't
> worry, it won't make your skin turn green!

Meg's Rose Water

Rose water is a gentle natural astringent which has
been popular in cosmetics for centuries. It's very
simple to make your own, it smells gorgeous, and it
suits a range of skin types. Some of the traditional
methods for making rose water are more involved,
but my friend's grandmother has been using this easy
version for years.

INGREDIENTS

1 cup rose petals (make sure the roses have not been
   sprayed)
2 cups boiling water
1 Tbsp gin or vodka (optional)

1) Place the petals in a heatproof bowl or jug, and cover
with the boiling water.

2) Cover the bowl or jug with a saucepan lid or
upturned dinner plate, and allow the petals to steep for
about half an hour.

3) Strain the liquid into a prepared jar, and leave it to
cool.

4) If you wish, add gin or vodka and mix by swirling
the jar around. This will make your rose water last
longer — up to a month or more, if stored in a cool
place.

> TIP: Some people say to leave it over-
> night, but if you just want to get going
> half an hour will still be effective.

5) Put rose water into a spritzer bottle for a refreshing and moisturising facial spray, or pat it directly onto your skin.

TIP: Mix rose water with glycerine (cup for cup) to make a simple, revitalising moisturiser. In pretty jars, this makes a lovely homemade gift.

Deb's Calendula Cream

Deb-the-midwife introduced me to this cream when our daughter was born, and it saw us through years of trouble-free nappies. I swear by it, and it's a favourite amongst parents. Anything to make nappy time a better place…

As well as protecting babies' bottoms, calendula is a natural healer with anti-inflammatory and anti-bacterial properties. Grown-ups can use the cream on dry skin, eczema, wounds, sprains, burns, bruises — anywhere really (well, anywhere external!) Growing calendula is also great for the garden (see p. 31), and it flowers profusely with bright gold petals — it's really worth planting your own, even if you only have pot space.

INGREDIENTS
250 g vegetable shortening (make sure it's 100 per cent vegetable, e.g. Kremelta)
1 Tbsp beeswax (grated)
½ cup calendula petals (dried)

1) Place the shortening and grated beeswax in a saucepan, and stir slowly over a low heat to melt together.

2) Stir in the dried calendula petals, squeezing them gently against the sides of the saucepan now and then to release the good stuff.

3) Pour into prepared glass jars and leave to cool before sealing.

TIP: Homemade calendula cream is a perfect gift for new parents — make a cute label or tie a ribbon around the jar and Bob's your uncle!

Free Fun for Kids

I grew up, as did my mother, in a small town in the middle of Zimbabwe. Being a teacher, Mum kept me busy throughout my preschool years with a catalogue of activities, from scrapbooking to sewing (I was a great disappointment when it came to the latter!) By the time my brother was a toddler, Mum had opened a small home-based kindergarten. It was busy and popular, and despite supplies being hard to come by there were always plenty of activities on offer. Taking something and re-using it to make something else is a necessity in third world countries — recycling comes naturally. Mum hoarded all kinds of household items, could fix an appliance with a piece of copper wire, and would whip off her stockings to create a makeshift fan belt if the car broke down (which it always did) mid road trip.

Now a nana herself, my mother has passed on her best toddler-taming tricks for me to use with my own daughter — and I hope they keep filtering down the generations. It's comforting feeling at least a tad environmentally friendly when playing with your kids, and always a bonus not having to set foot inside a plastic-o-rama toy store. These ideas require little or no money, use easy-to-find materials, and can entertain your hyperactive little monkeys for hours without them even remembering the telly.

flour and water glue

This takes thirty seconds to make and is entirely non-toxic.

INGREDIENTS
a little cold water
2 Tbsp flour (adjust amount to suit)
kid's paintbrush

1) Slowly add the cold water to the flour, stirring throughout, until you have a thick, smooth paste.

2) You just made glue!

Even small children can apply this glue with a paint brush, and it won't matter if it ends up in their mouths. Use it for making homemade cards and pictures, or let your child loose with a magazine and some scissors…

TIP: Don't underestimate the sticking power of Flour and Water Glue – it sets like concrete! Mum still has pictures – intact – that I made with it two (ok, three) decades ago. Wash the bowl of glue with hot water when the kids are done, or you'll end up chiselling it out later.

mosaics

INGREDIENTS

old magazines, used greeting cards, old books, etc.
kid-friendly scissors
flour and water glue
plain paper

1) Kids love cutting and sticking. Let them spend as long as they like finding pictures, cutting them out and pasting them onto paper, to make mosaic creations.

2) With toddlers it's usually best to go freestyle, but older kids often enjoy more structure. Draw the outline of a fish and get them to cut out coloured and patterned pieces to make scales. Or draw the outline of a butterfly, pirate ship or alien monster and let them decorate it collage-style.

potato stamps

INGREDIENTS

kid-safe paint
kitchen sponge
a little flour (optional)
potatoes
plain paper

A little paint squeezed onto a kitchen sponge makes an excellent stamp pad. Spread the paint onto the sponge with a spoon and it's ready to use. Add a little flour to the paint to thicken it if necessary.

The humble potato can be turned into an effective stamp, and it's a great way of using up potatoes that are past their eat-by date. Of course if you're growing your own (p. 38), it helps take care of any excess crop!

1) Cut a potato in half lengthwise.

2) Cut a simple shape in the centre of the potato with your knife, e.g. a square, triangle or diamond.

3) Remove the flesh around the shape so that the shape itself protrudes.

4) Voilà, a stamp! Show your kids how to press the potato onto the sponge, then stamp it onto the paper.

5) Smaller children will stamp shapes all over the show, while older kids can make pictures — such as a simple house, train, etc. — using different basic shapes. They'll have loads of fun and learn early mathematics principles at the same time, without realising.

homemade play dough

Play dough is pricey to buy but easy and quick to make at home. This is a simple recipe using ingredients from the pantry.

INGREDIENTS

2 cups flour
1 cup salt
1 cup water
2 tsp Cream of Tartar (optional)
1 Tbsp oil (any cooking oil will work)
food colouring (optional)

1) Mix all the ingredients together in a bowl (except the food colouring), adding the oil last.

2) Knead the dough until it feels good — the kids can help with this.

3) Add a few drops of food colouring to make coloured dough, or split into batches and make different colours.

4) Store in airtight containers.

TIP: If you're out of potatoes, the stamp pad can be used with all kinds of objects. An upturned cup will make a circle, used cotton reels make great patterns, etc. — get creative with your recycling pile. Plastic biscuit cutters (smooth side down) are also a favourite.

paper creations

INGREDIENT
paper

It's amazing what you can do with just one piece of paper. Even if that's all you've got in the house, there's still fun to be had.

paper planes

Paper planes have been a childhood staple for generations of kids. I was embarrassed to discover recently that I didn't know how to fold one properly, so if you're like me don't tell your kids — here's the low-down:

1) Take a piece of rectangular paper (such as A4 photocopier paper) and fold it in half lengthwise.

2) Holding the crease closest to you, fold the top right corner down so it lines up with the bottom — forming a small triangle shape at one end.

3) Turn over and repeat on the other side.

4) Take the top crease you've just formed, and fold it down to meet the bottom crease.

5) Turn over and repeat.

6) You now have an even longer crease at the top. Fold this down to meet the bottom too.

7) Repeat overleaf.

8) Lock your wings up into position, and fly, fly, fly!

hand holders

1) Take a rectangular piece of paper and fold the bottom up a couple of centimetres. Crease well.

2) Turn the paper over so the crease is now at the top, and the folded bit underneath.

3) Take the top crease and fold it down the same distance as your first fold.

4) Repeat until you've folded the whole piece of paper, creating a wide fan.

5) With paper folded, draw a simple outline of a person lengthwise on one edge. Make sure the arms extend as far as the sides and end at the 'wrists'.

6) Get your child to cut carefully around the shape, except for the 'wrists' at the sides.

7) Open out the folds of paper and you'll have a line of people holding hands.

TIP: Older kids may enjoy drawing faces and clothes on the people to create different characters.

wish picker

1) Begin with a piece of square paper.

2) Fold paper in half along both diagonals to make creases. The point where these creases meet is the centre of the paper.

3) Fold each corner of the paper into the centre.

4) Turn the whole piece of paper over, and fold these corners into the centre too.

5) Take the bottom of your now smaller square and fold it in half to meet the top.

6) Reach the thumb and forefinger of each hand under the paper flaps, and push your hands together until the paper meets in the middle. You should now find you can open and shut your wish picker by moving your fingers.

7) Younger kids enjoy sticking their fingers in the middle and tempting you to catch them like a Venus flytrap.

8) Older children can write numbers or draw colours on each of the inner flaps, and write messages or wishes underneath for their friends to pick.

binoculars

You can't beat a toilet roll for entertainment! Intrepid explorers and young would-be hunters love these binoculars.

INGREDIENTS

2 toilet rolls (if you're squeamish about using toilet rolls, cut a paper towel inner in half)
paint (optional)
Sellotape
string or wool

1) Get your child to paint the toilet rolls if they wish.

2) Once dry, Sellotape them together, side by side.

3) Cut a length of string or wool and Sellotape each end to the sides of the toilet rolls to create a neck strap.

4) Take your explorer with their binoculars to the park or zoo — they'll be convinced they can see things more clearly!

TIP: Tie a knot in each end of the string or wool before you attach it to prevent it being pulled through the Sellotape.

freestyling

INGREDIENTS
toilet rolls
cardboard boxes
miles and miles of Sellotape

1) Let your kids loose with these ingredients.

2) They can spend hours and hours constructing houses, robots, space ships and strange, unidentifiable objects.

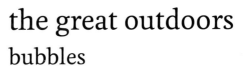

the great outdoors
bubbles

INGREDIENTS
dishwashing liquid
water
paper clip

Bubbles are fun, even grown-ups think so! But commercial bubble mix is expensive for what it is, and it's easy to make your own.

1) Simply mix a little dishwashing liquid with cold water, at a ratio of about 1 tsp dishwashing liquid to 3 tsp water (experiment to find the perfect balance).

2) Pour this onto a small plate or dish.

3) Make a bubble wand by un-bending a paper clip, and folding it back on itself to create a loop. Dip it in the bubble mix and blow!

kaleidoscope

INGREDIENTS
shiny chocolate wrappers (or similar)
kid-friendly scissors
greaseproof paper (or baking paper)
1 toilet roll (or paper towel inner)

1) Get your small darling to cut a bunch of chocolate wrappers (or other shiny paper) into bits. Or do it yourself — it's very therapeutic!

2) Sandwich these shiny paper bits between two squares of baking paper, and Sellotape the whole thing on to the end of a toilet roll. You just got yourself a kaleidoscope!

3) Hold it up to the light and twist it round slowly to see the pretty patterns. Now stop, and give your child a go!

seed sprouting

This was a favourite of mine as a kid.

INGREDIENTS
cotton wool balls
empty egg carton
bean seeds

1) Place a cotton wool ball in each of the carton's egg spaces.

2) 'Plant' a bean seed on top of each, and cover with another cotton ball.

3) Leave in a warm spot (such as a sunny windowsill), and get your child to water gently each day.

4) Check the seeds' progress by lifting the top cotton wool ball to see them. Bean seeds sprout quickly, so they won't disappoint the impatient!

5) Transplant the sprouts into a pot or garden once they're growing well.

Mum says: 'It's a good idea to put a tray or towel under the egg carton in case the water soaks through.' Yes Mum.

mini garden

INGREDIENTS
small container (e.g. empty ice cream container)
soil or sand

1) Fill the container with a little soil or sand, and give it to the kids to create their own 'garden'.

2) They can hunt in the backyard or park or on the beach for leaves, sticks, flowers, shells, etc. with which to create their garden. You'll be surprised how long it keeps them busy!

Mum says: 'It sounds so simple, but this one is an absolute winner every time.'

TIP: Make a slow-flo watering can by poking holes in the lid of an empty plastic milk bottle with a needle, or hammer and nail.

BIRTHDAY HUH ?

Kylie's
Cards and Envelopes

There's a long tradition of treasure-hunting in Kylie Sutcliffe's family, and as a kid she prided herself on being the champion. She always had her eyes on the kerb, seeking out coins, buttons and anything shiny. The only one to outdo Kylie was her Scottish Grandpa, who took being frugal to a whole new level. His creative DIY efforts were almost entirely constructed from found items, and for as long as he lived he steamed off any stamps without a postmark to be used over again.

Kylie has always had a fascination with paper, and its different designs and textures. One Christmas her Aunty Anne gave her a paper bag stacked full of smaller paper bags of various types and colours. It remains one of Kylie's favourite gifts ever!

Greeting cards are surprisingly expensive, and a handmade one is always special. They're personal, and can be tailored to suit the recipient. You can make them as complicated as you like, and spend hours getting arty, but they can be equally effective when kept simple. Kylie reckons anyone can whip up a card and envelope in less time than it takes to get out to the shop and buy one.

making a card

These instructions are for making a simple card, with a cardboard outer and plain paper inner: book style.

INGREDIENTS
• cardstock — card that's thick enough to stand up on its own when folded, so your creation can be displayed. It needn't be of the highest quality. There are lots of colours on offer — check your local stationery store
• materials for your design — pictures, ephemera, photographs, pens, pencils, glue, scissors and whatever else you might use to create the look you want
• plain paper (optional) — anything you can write on will do. Check the recycling pile next to the printer or photocopier.
• needle and thread (optional) — this is for attaching the plain paper to the cardboard outer. Kylie suggests a large needle and thick thread, such as embroidery cotton, string or a thin ribbon

Kylie says: 'Keep an eye out for things you can recycle, like old manila folders.'

1) Make the card outer first. Decide what size and shape you want your card to be — square, tall and thin, short and squat — and cut a piece of cardstock to double that size. Fold it in half. Your card has a skeleton!

TIP: If you intend to make lots of cards it's worth getting a pack of cardstock to have on hand.

127

Kylie says: 'My favourite shape is a tall thin card, they look great when displayed.'

2) Now's the time to get as creative as you like with your design. Your card can be simple, elegant, funny — or you can even use newspaper images for a bit of satire. Stick stuff on, draw, paint — whatever takes your fancy. You could mount a photograph or picture on the inside of your card by cutting four diagonal slots to poke the corners into. Using a craft knife or other sharp knife, cut a window in the front of your card, so only part of the image shows through.

Kylie says: 'If in doubt I keep it simple — I just choose an image the person will like and stick it on.'

TIP: If you stick images onto your card, it's a good idea to dry the card underneath a stack of heavy books to flatten out any warping or bubbles. Place it between layers of greaseproof or baking paper to stop it sticking to the books. If you've left it till the last minute and the birthday dinner starts now, don't panic - warping adds character.

3) Next, make the inner. Cut your piece of plain paper a few millimetres shorter and narrower than your card, so it sits snugly inside.

4) Position the paper inside the card and use your needle to poke two holes at the fold. The holes should pierce both the paper and cardstock behind it, and occur at equal distances from the top and bottom.

5) Thread the needle, and pass it through one hole and up into the other. Pull the needle off the thread, and tie the two loose ends together in a knot. You can choose to have your knot and thread tails on the outside or the inside of the card. For a knot on the outside, start and finish with your needle on the outside, and vice versa.

TIP: If that's taking you past your be-bothered threshold, simply glue the plain paper onto the inside of the card, or skip this step altogether and write directly on the cardstock.

6) Write the message! Tell them all the wonderful things you most appreciate about them and how much you love them. Or ask them for that twenty bucks they borrowed (include a stamped, self-addressed envelope). Or whatever.

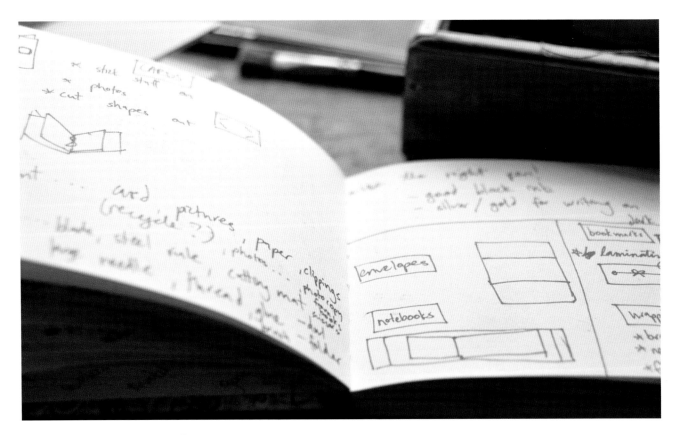

making an envelope

INGREDIENTS
cardstock
hole punch
ribbon, string or thread

1) Place your card lengthwise in the middle of another piece of cardstock.

2) Fold the long sides (only) of the cardstock around your card. Trim the cardstock if necessary to avoid the sides overlapping too much, but make sure the ends extend a centimetre or so beyond each end of your card.

3) Punch a single hole in each end of the envelope, i.e. the bits that extend beyond your card. Be careful not to catch your card in the middle! The hole should pierce both the overlapping sides and back of the envelope.

4) Thread a thin piece of ribbon, string or pretty thread through each hole and tie securely in a knot or bow. Your card is trapped!

5) These envelopes are secure enough to send through the mail — just pop a stamp on (or steam one off another envelope if you're Scottishly-inclined like Kylie's Grandpa).

Quilting has been a popular nana sport since, it seems, the dawn of time. Or, at least, the dawn of needles. These days the trend is enjoying a renaissance, and spreading its joy far beyond nana circles. You can take quilting as far as you like, inventing patterns and designs and winning top awards like Clare Smith. But, even if this is not your cup of tea, a simple quilt is still achievable — and hugely satisfying.

Clare's love of quilting began as a child growing up in Kenya. There was no TV, so Clare took up a needle and thread to entertain herself. She went on to become a leading quilting instructor, and has plenty of great tips for beginners — even impatient, non-crafty types like me. Now you'll know what to do when there's nothing good on TV!

beginner's patchwork quilt

INGREDIENTS

pieces of fabric for patches
cardboard
piece of backing fabric, roughly the size you want your
    quilt to be
batting (synthetic, fluffy fabric you can buy cheaply
    from a fabric store — optional)
needles
cotton thread
embroidery thread
buttons (optional)

1) Choose the fabrics you want to use on your quilt.
Patchwork quilting is a great excuse to chop up tired
clothes and re-use them.

2) Prewash all fabrics, and dry well. Iron them all. (Yes,
you do have to.)

Clare says: 'Even if you never usually pick
up an iron, promise not to skip this step!
Un-ironed material is hard to work with,
and will affect the shape of the quilt.'

3) Decide on a size for the squares you plan to use on
your quilt, and cut a piece of cardboard to fit this shape.
The cardboard will be your template.

4) Using the cardboard template, cut your chosen
fabrics into identically sized squares. The number of
squares you need will depend on the size of the quilt
you want to make.

TIP: Use a ruler and measure the square
carefully, so the sides are straight and
even.

Clare says: 'Cut your fabric so that the grain
runs straight up the square, not diagonally
across, or your quilt will be all bendy.'

5) Lay out your squares side by side to form a large
rectangle. When they make a pattern that you like, take
a photo so you remember the order, or place the layout
somewhere it won't be disturbed.

6) Take the 9 squares that form the top left-hand corner of your rectangle. This will be your first 'block'.

7) Fold the first square patch over its neighbour so they face each other, right side inwards. Line up the edges.

8) Using a simple running stitch, sew down one side of the square about ½ cm from the edge to join the patches together. Backstitch at the beginning and end of the seam to secure it.

▬▬ ▬ ▬ ▬ ▬ ▬ ▬ ▬ ▬ ▬ ▬

• *Running stitch*: This is a very simple stitch that runs in a straight line. Pass a threaded needle up through your fabrics, then down again a few millimetres along. This is your first stitch. Leave a small gap, then bring the needle up again, and down as before — keeping this second stitch the same length as the first. Continue along the fabric as far as you need to.

• *Backstitch*: Pass a threaded needle up through the fabrics, then down again a few millimetres back towards you. Pass it up again a few millimetres in front of the first stitch, and down where that stitch began.

▬▬ ▬ ▬ ▬ ▬ ▬ ▬ ▬ ▬ ▬ ▬

9) Sew the adjoining seams of each of the 9 patches in this way, until your block is complete.

TIP: If you have a sewing machine (and know how to use it!) you can machine sew the seams instead. Make sure the seam is only half a centimetre wide – this is different from a dressmaker's seam. Don't backstitch or break the thread when you get to the end – instead, continue straight on to the next squares in the block.

10) Repeat with the next set of 9 squares until all the patches of your quilt are in blocks.

11) Sew down the adjoining seams to attach the blocks to each other.

12) The patchwork 'top' — the most difficult part of your quilt — is now complete. Lay down the fabric you want on the back of your quilt, covered by quilt batting fabric if desired, and place your patchwork 'top' on top.

13) Trim the lower two layers to the same size as the top.

TIP: Choose a heavier fabric for the back, such as polar fleece, for a cosy quilt which doesn't need batting. Don't use polar fleece on babies' quilts, however, as they can over-heat underneath it. Avoid using wool, as this can change shape when washed.

14) Line up the patchwork top over the backing fabric and batting, right sides facing inwards. Pin it in place to make sure the sides stay lined up.

15) Sew a seam all the way up one side, across the top, and down the other side — but do not sew across the bottom.

16) Once your seams are complete, trim the batting down close to the seam, and turn the quilt right side out (pull through the bottom opening).

17) To close the quilt, fold the edges of the bottom seam inwards and pin in place. Sew along the bottom seam to hem.

18) You now have the makings of a very simple patchwork quilt! Complete it by using ties or buttons to join ('quilt') the two sides together.

•*Ties*: This is a simple method of quilting your quilt. Choose a coloured, stranded embroidery thread to suit your quilt. Thread it through a large needle, and pass the needle down through all the layers of your quilt. Bring it back up again about 2 mm away. Unthread the needle, and tie the two loose ends together. Repeat this process all over the quilt, at regular or random intervals, keeping the ties no more than 10 cm apart, so the layers will stay together well, especially when washed.

•*Buttons*: You can also quilt in a similar way using buttons. Choose interesting buttons and sew them onto your quilt, through all the layers, at regular or random intervals as per the ties. Pass the needle up through all the layers and through one hole of the button. Bring it back down through the opposite hole of the button and the layers of fabric. Repeat until the button is secure. Finish with a backstitch on the under layer of the fabric. (Don't use buttons if the quilt is for a child under three years old.)

TIP: Quilts are a fabulous way to recycle old clothes, like those worn-out pyjamas you love but which you should really move on from! A good quilt can even become a family heir-loom, incorporating bits of fabric from each member of the family.

Tribute to Nanas

Index

Make your own kaleidoscope, see p. 123.

Robyn Paterson

ROBYN PATERSON is a television writer, director and producer with a wide range of credits, from children's shows to satire, documentary to commercials. Robyn started independent film company Walking On Air Productions in 2004, and its two niche short films have won five festival awards and a US television deal between them. Robyn is currently directing a documentary produced by Leanne Pooley (director of *The Topp Twins — Untouchable Girls*). In *Tips from your Nana*, her first book, Robyn draws on her documentary experience and gathers gems of wisdom along the way.

TAMMY WILLIAMS was born in Johannesburg, South Africa, where she lived until the tender age of thirteen. She had a passion for photography from a young age which she continues to nurture. She is currently based in Wellington, New Zealand, where she works in the film and TV industry.